W9-CHX-149

Seminar
Notebook

A resource designed to supplement
the Creation Seminar Series

Dr. Kent Hovind

CSE Ministry

Top row: Paul Jewell, Eric, and Kent Andrew
Middle row: Marlissa Jewell, Tanya, Danielle
Dr. Kent Hovind and Mrs. Jo Hovind
Bottom row: Angelina, Matthew, Kailey, and Stephanie

INTRODUCTION

This notebook is designed to accompany the seven videotapes or DVD's of my Creation Seminar Series. Though not designed to be read from cover to cover like most books, much interesting reading can be found here. Most charts, graphs, and sources to which I refer in my seminars are included in this book, as well as an extensive frequently-asked-questions section near the end. New materials are constantly being added to make this notebook a handy reference tool. Remember, none of my material is restricted. This is by design. For years I have said, "There is a war going on. You don't ration out bullets during war time!" If you can shoot and want to use my "bullets," feel free to do so. It is my prayer that all of our materials will renew your confidence in the Word of God and inspire you to serve the Lord with your life, or draw you to the Lord if you are not saved.

We also offer a fill-in-the-blank Seminar Workbook as a supplement for those who may want to use our award winning Creation Seminar Series as a class. For those who really want to learn about the creation subject our college courses CS 101- CS 104 may be just what you need. See our catalog, web site, or contact the office for details.

CSE Ministry
Kent Hovind (Hō-vînd)
29 Cummings Rd
Pensacola, FL [32503]
850-479-3466
1-877-479-3466 (USA only)
850-479-8562 Fax
dino@drdino.com
www.drdino.com

Copyright © 2006 by CSE Ministry.
Permission is granted to duplicate for free distribution only.

ISBN 1-58468-018-0

DEDICATION

This Seminar Notebook is dedicated to my loving wife, Jo. Without her support and tireless efforts, the ministry of Creation Science Evangelism would not be here today.

On July 14th 2003, Jo and I celebrated our 30th anniversary! We sat down and figured out how much money we have spent in the last 30 years. It really didn't take long. We have spent all of it (and then some)!

When I was just a few minutes old (a while ago!), my mother folded her hands over mine and prayed for God to provide a godly wife for me some day. Boy, did He answer that prayer! Jo and I began dating when she was just a freshman in high school (I was a cool senior!). I had been invited to share my testimony at her church youth group in Peoria, Illinois on October 4, 1970, where I saw her for the first time. The next day, I invited her to a youth activity I was going to that evening and she accepted! On the way home my 1963 VW broke down. We tried to find a house with a phone, but to no avail, so I said, "Let's pray." I asked the Lord to make the car run one more time so I could get her home on time. When I turned the key it started and ran four more miles to her house and quit again! (I should have asked the Lord to fix it for good!) My first date cost me over $400 and it was worth every penny! God answered our prayer on that first date and has answered thousands more since then.

We have been very active in God's work since before we met and God has brought us through everything just like He promises in Matthew 6:33. Jo has been a key helper, as our ministry has grown from nothing to one of the largest creation ministries in the world. We have an awesome staff of about 40 and a worldwide influence with literally millions of our videos in circulation and changing lives since 1989.

God has given us three wonderful children. All are married, living around us, giving us lots of grandkids and all working in the ministry with us.

In 1993, Jo finished her Master's degree in music. She is an incredible vocalist, pianist, teacher, wife, mother, and cook and is the hardest working woman I have ever seen. She memorized Proverbs 31 as a teen and has come the closest to being that virtuous woman that I have ever met. She has given up her house (we have had ten ministry offices in our house for years), as well as given up her husband to travel (I have been gone over 200 days most years) and, yet, she keeps a cheerful spirit while working for the Lord. I am truly the most blessed man on earth to have a wife like her! Hopefully, God will give us 30 more years together. Thanks, Jo, for loving the Lord first and then me.

"It cannot be emphasized too strongly or too often that this great nation was founded not by religionists but by Christians... not on religions but on the Gospel of Jesus Christ."
—Patrick Henry

"It is impossible to rightly govern...without God and the Bible"
—George Washington

"If we abide by the principles taught in the Bible, our country will go on prospering, but if we neglect its instruction and authority, no man can tell how soon a catastrophe may overcome us, and bury all our glory in profound obscurity.
—Daniel Webster

Table of Contents

2004 EDITION

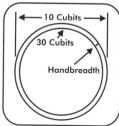

Miscellaneous (Green pages)

Frequently Asked Questions (Yellow pages)

Reference Lists (Blue pages)

Charts (Fold-out pages)

Sci•ence \ ˈsī-ən(t)s \ n [ME, fr. MF, fr. L scientia, fr. scient-, sciens having knowledge, fr. prp. of scire to know; prob. akin to Skt chyati he cuts off, L sciendere to split — more at SHED] (14c)   **1**: the state of knowing : knowledge as distinguished from ignorance or misunderstanding   **2 a**: a department of systematized knowledge as an object of study ⟨ the ~ of theology⟩   **b**: something (as a sport or technique) that may be studied or learned like systematized knowledge ⟨have it down to a ~⟩   **3 a**: knowledge or a system of knowledge covering general truths or the operation of general laws esp. as obtained and tested through scientific method   **b**: such knowledge or such a system of knowledge concerned with the physical world and its phenomena : NATURAL SCIENCE   **4**: a system or method reconciling practical ends with scientific laws ⟨culinary ~⟩   **5** cap: CHRISTIAN SCIENCE

From Merriam-Webster's Collegiate® Dictionary, Tenth Edition
©2003 by Merriam-Webster, Incorporated (www.Merriam-

Seminar Outline
Major Points Covered in the Video Series by Dr. Kent Hovind

Part 1A—Big Bang, Big Dud

- Four great questions every religion tries to answer.
  - Who am I?
  - Where did I come from?
  - Why am I here?
  - Where am I going when I die?
- Two irreconcilable worldviews:
  - Creation
  - Evolution
- Satan's lie to Eve
  - Masked his own desire to be God
  - Began his 6,000 year attempt to destroy humanity
  - Began a false worldview of evolving to godhood
- Big lies are believed more easily than small ones
- Effectual lies are mixed with truth
- Technique used in advertising
- Modern science textbooks mix evolution and science
- Textbooks confuse six types of evolution
  - Cosmic evolution (Big Bang - origin of matter)
  - Chemical evolution (higher chemical)
  - Planetary and stellar evolution (origin of the stars)
  - Organic evolution (origin of life)
  - Macroevolution - animals changing into new kinds(unobserved)
  - Microevolution (variation)
- Fairytales are taught in school
  - Frog + kiss = prince
  - Frog + time = prince
- Evidence against the Big Bang
- Evolution violates both laws of thermodynamics
- Students are taught they are animals
- Many students behave like animals
- Teachers can teach creation in public schools
- Decline in morals since 1963
- Scientists have a long history of being wrong
- Majority of Americans do not believe in evolution
- Belief in evolution will destroy confidence in Scripture

Part 1B—The Age of the Earth

- Proofs of a young universe and Earth
  - Earth's population
  - Spinning galaxies
  - Earth's magnetic field
  - Earth's rotational speed

"Martin Lingis is probably right in saying that 'more cases of loss of religious faith are to be traced to the theory of evolution...than to anything else.'"
—**Huston Smith** "Evolution & Evolutionism" *Christian Century* July 1982, p. 755

"...researchers suggest that virtually all modern men—99.9% of them, says one scientist—are closely related genetically and share genes with one male ancestor, dubbed 'Y-chromosome Adam.'

"We are finding that humans have very, very shallow genetic roots which go back very recently to one ancestor, ...that indicates that there was an origin in a specific location on the globe, and then it spread out from there."
—**U.S. News & World Report,** December 4, 1995

Note: We knew this before and we even knew his name! Adam.

- Underground oil pressure
- Ice cores in Greenland & Antarctica
- Mississippi River delta
- Methuselah tree
- Great Barrier Reef
- Niagara Falls
- Ocean salinity
- Stalactite & stalagmite formation
- Short period comets
- Continental erosion
- Oldest writings and languages

Part 2—The Garden of Eden

- People who scoff at the Bible are "willingly ignorant" of the creation and the flood
- Originally created world was different
- Gap Theory
- Day-Age Theory
- Pre-flood water canopy
    - Why people lived to be over 900 years old
    - Why dinosaurs grew so big
    - Hyperbaric chamber
- Cave Men
    - Nebraska Man
    - Piltdown Man
    - Neanderthal Man
    - Lucy
- Huge animals and plants lived before the flood
- Dinosaurs lived with man before the flood
- God's original diet
- God's promise to restore the earth

Part 3A—Dinosaurs and the Bible

- Dinosaurs on the Ark
- Flood Legends
- Noah's Ark discovered? —two possibilities
- Most dinosaurs died shortly after the flood
    - Different climate
    - Man's hunting
- Dinosaurs in history
- Dinosaurs mentioned in the Bible

Part 3B—Dinosaurs Today

- Could a few dinosaurs still be alive?
- Thousands of sightings in remote places
    - Mokele-Mbembe in Africa
    - Loch Ness
    - Japanese catch

"'Science' in its deep and original sense means *knowledge*. We discover by hard work what is knowledge and what is not. And there are no philosophical shortcuts to that end."
—J. P. Moreland, *Bible-Science News,* volume 32:6

"I am much afraid that the schools will prove to be the great gates to Hell unless they diligently labor in explaining the Scriptures, engraving them in the hearts of youth. I advise no one to place his child where the scriptures do not reign paramount. Every institution in which men are not increasingly occupied with the Word of God, must become corrupt."
—Martin Luther

"L. Tiger, an anthropologist at Rutgers, contends that Darwinian science inevitably will, and should have legal, political and moral consequences..."
—Scientific American, October 1995, p. 181

"Other examples, including the much-repeated 'gradual' evolution of the modern horse, have not held up under close examination."
—**Biology** *The Unity and diversity of Life* Wadsworth 1992 P. 304

Problems with Horse Evolution:

1. Made up by Othniel C. Marsh in 1874 from fossils scattered across the world, not from same location.
2. Modern horses are found in layers with and lower than "ancient horses". Kruzhilin, Yu, and V. Ovcharov, "A Horse from the Dinosaur Epoch?" *Moskovskaya Pravda* (*"Moscow Truth"*), trans. A. James Melnick (February 5, 1984).
3. The "ancient horse" (hyracotherium) is not a horse but is just like the hyrax still alive in Turkey and Madagascar today!
4. Ribs, toes and teeth are different.
5. South American fossils go from 1 toed to 3 toed.
6. Never found in order presented.
—See **Frank Sherwin** of ICR for more. ICR.ORG

- China
- California
- Canada
- Lake Champlain, Vermont
- Off the coast of Pensacola, Florida

Part 4—Lies in the Textbooks?

- Public school textbooks are one of the main tools used to turn students away from Christianity.
- Many "proofs" for evolution were disproved years ago—and are still in the textbooks.
  - Grand Canyon formed fast
  - Vestigial organs (walking whales)
  - The Geologic Column uses circular reasoning
  - Macroevolution assumed
  - Mutations do not improve a species or create new ones
  - Peppered Moth
  - Horse Evolution
  - Life in the lab
  - Small does not mean simple
- Parents need to be alert against brainwashing
- Students should look for alternative explanations for what we observe in nature
  - Common bone structure in fore limbs.
  - Common Ancestor?
  - Common Designer!

Part 5—The Dangers of Evolution

- Things parents and students can do:
  - Encourage textbook selection committees and school boards to follow laws requiring textbooks to be accurate
  - Remove false material from textbooks Options to take until new books can be purchased:
    - Cut out or black out false information.
    - Glue pages together if they have false information.
    - Place warning stickers in the front of each book.
    - Give students booklets detailing errors.
    - Get on textbook selection committees.
    - Get book publishers to print error-free editions for your district.
- Do not confront teachers publicly
- Many students allow teachers and classmates to watch our video series on creation
- The Origin of Species made the world worse

"Socialism is the gospel of envy, the creed of ignorance, and the philosophy of failure."
—**Winston Churchill**

"Isn't the only hope for the planet that the industrialized civilizations collapse? Isn't it our responsibility to bring that about?"
—**Maurice Strong,** Head of 1992 Earth Summit, Rio de Janeiro

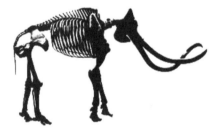

- Satan's lie rehashed
- Many men based their destructive philosophies on evolution:
  - Adolf Hitler
  - Joseph Stalin
  - Pol Pot
  - Benito Mussolini
  - John D. Rockefeller
- They use evolution as an excuse to enslave others
- Only one solution: II Chronicles 7:14

Part 6—The Hovind Theory

- The myth of Pangea
- Cause of the worldwide flood
- Ice Age and how it fits in with the Bible
- How the Grand Canyon was formed
- Origin of coal, natural gas, oil, limestone, etc.
- Ice Meteor Theory
  - Break up in space and deflected by Earth's magnetic field
  - Lands in polar regions
  - Instant Ice Age
  - Frozen mammoths
  - Cracks in the Earth's crust
- Earth flooded by three sources:
  1. Water from pre-flood canopy
  2. "Fountains of the deep" breaking up
  3. Ice meteor from space
- Dead animals deposited and turned to fossils, oil and natural gas
- Huge forests buried and turned to coal
- Mountains lifted up (Psalm 104)
- Grand Canyon formed
- Geologic features explained

Part 7—Question and Answer Session

- Explanation for billions of light-years from stars
- Supposed contradictions in the Bible
- Carbon Dating
- Where did the races come from?
- Why KJV?
- Great Pyramid
- Does God get old?
- Bigfoot
- UFOs
- Much more!

ARTICLES

"One cannot be exposed to the law and order of the universe without concluding that there must be design and purpose behind it all.... To be forced to believe only one conclusion— that everything in the universe happened by chance—would violate the very objectivity of science itself.... They (evolutionists) challenge science to prove the existence of God. But must we really light a candle to see the sun? It is in scientific honesty that I endorse the presentation of alternative theories for the origin of the universe, life and man in the science classroom. It would be an error to overlook the possibility that the universe was planned rather than happening by chance."

—Dr. Wernher von Braun
(Father of American rocket and space program)

Dr. Hovind's $250,000 Offer
Offered Since 1990–Increased from $10,000 in 1999

I have a standing offer of $250,000 to anyone who can give any empirical evidence (scientific proof) for evolution.* My $250,000 offer demonstrates that the hypothesis of evolution is nothing more than a man-made belief system (religion).

Observed phenomena:

Most thinking people will agree that:

1. A highly ordered universe exists.
2. At least one planet (probably only one) in this complex universe contains an amazing variety of life forms.
3. Man appears to be the most advanced form of life on this planet.

Known options:

Choices of how the observed phenomena came into being:

1. The universe was created by God.
2. The universe always existed.
3. The universe came into being by itself by purely natural processes (known as evolution) so that no appeal to the supernatural is needed.

Students in tax-supported schools are being taught that evolution is a fact. We are convinced that evolution is a religion masquerading as science and should not be part of any science curriculum. It has nothing to do with the subject of science. There are at least six different and unrelated meanings to the word "evolution." Students are deceived into thinking all six types of evolution below have been proven because evidence is given for minor variations called Microevolution.

1. Cosmic evolution—the origin of time, space, and matter. Big Bang.
2. Chemical evolution—the origin of higher elements from hydrogen.
3. Stellar and planetary evolution—origin of stars and planets.
4. Organic evolution—origin of life from inanimate matter.
5. Macroevolution—changing from one kind into another.
6. Microevolution—variations within kinds. Only this one has been observed.

This deception is a classic bait and switch. One definition of evolution (descent with modification) is given, and the others are assumed to be true by association. The first five meanings are believed by faith and are religious. Only the last one is scientific.

* NOTE:
When I use the word evolution, I am not referring to the minor variations found in all of the various life forms (microevolution). I am referring to the general theory of evolution which believes these five major events took place without God:

- 1. Time, space, and matter came into existence by themselves.
- 2. Planets and stars formed from space dust.
- 3. Matter created life by itself.
- 4. Early life forms learned to reproduce themselves.
- 5. Major changes occurred between these diverse life forms (i.e., fish changed to amphibians, amphibians changed to reptiles, and reptiles changed to birds or mammals).

"In fact, evolution became in a sense a scientific religion; almost all scientists have accepted it, and many are prepared to 'bend' their observations to fit with it."
—**H. S. Lipson**, FRS, Professor of Physics, University of Manchester, UK in "A Physicist Looks at Evolution," *Physics Bulletin,* vol. 31 (May, 1980), p. 138

Make sure to see Dr. Hovind's new video series, *Dr. Hovind answers his critics.*

There are nearly 1000 "anti-Hovind" web sites. See and hear Dr. Hovind's response in this eight hour series. Available from CSE $45.00.

The Altogether Missing Evidence: For Evolution

1. No evolution at present
2. No new species
3. No known mechanism of evolution
4. No fossil evidence
5. No recapitulation or vestigial organs

Empirical: relying, or based solely on experiment and observation, rather than theory.

Webster's New World Dictionary, 2nd College Edition

People do not know that evolution is true; yet, they believe in it. While beliefs are certainly fine to have, it is not fair nor legal to force on the students in our public school system the teaching of one belief, at taxpayers' expense. It is my contention that evolutionism is a religious worldview that is not supported by science, Scripture, popular opinion, or common sense. The exclusive teaching of this dangerous, mind-altering philosophy in tax-supported schools, parks, museums, etc., is a clear violation of the First Amendment.

How to collect the $250,000:

Prove beyond reasonable doubt that the process of evolution (option 3, pg. 2) is the only possible way the observed phenomena could have come into existence.

Only empirical evidence is acceptable. Persons wishing to collect the $250,000 may submit their evidence in writing or schedule time for a public presentation. A committee of trained scientists will provide peer review of the evidence offered and, to the best of their ability, will be fair and honest in their evaluation and judgment as to the validity of the evidence presented.

If you are convinced that evolution is an indisputable fact, may I suggest that you offer $250,000 for any empirical or historical evidence *against* the general theory of evolution. This might include the following:

- The earth is not billions of years old (thus destroying the possibility of evolution having happened as is taught).
- No animal has ever been observed changing into any fundamentally different kind of animal.
- No one has ever observed life spontaneously arising from nonliving matter.
- Matter cannot make itself out of nothing.

My suggestion:

Proponents of the theory of evolution would do well to admit that they **believe** in evolution, but they do not **know** if it happened the way they have been taught. They should call evolution their "faith" or "religion," and stop including it in books of science. I recommend that you not trust evolutionism, but in the God of the Bible, (the Creator of this universe and who will be our Judge one day soon) to forgive you and to save you from the coming judgment of man's sin.

Universe Not "Billions of Years Old"

Facts & Proof From Science

"Transformism (Evolution) is a fairy tale for grownups.
—**Jean Rostand,** Age Nouveau, [a French periodical] February 1959, p.12

"This theory has helped nothing in the progress of science. It is useless."
—**Professor Louis Bounoure,** Former President, Biological Society of Strasbourg, Director of the Strasbourg Zoological Museum, France Determinism and Finality, 1957, p. 79

"Evolution is unproved and unprovable. We believe it only because the only alternative is special creation, and that is unthinkable."
—**Sir Arthur Keith**

The general theory of evolution is based on several faulty assumptions. (Note: It is important to understand by this statement that we are not disputing simple variations that some call "microevolution," whose micro-changes are often observed but never lead to a fundamentally different kind of plant or animal.) The following assumptions of evolutionary theory are easily proven false:

- the universe is billions of years old,
- life spontaneously arose from nonliving minerals,
- mutations create or improve a species,
- natural selection has creative power.

In this section we will deal with the first of these assumptions. The others will be dealt with elsewhere. If, in fact, it could be demonstrated that the universe is not billions of years old, all other arguments about evolution become meaningless and unnecessary.

In children's fairy tales, we are told:

frog + magic spell (usually a kiss) = **prince**

In modern "science" textbooks we are told:

frog + time = prince

The same basic fairy tale is being promoted in textbooks today, but the new magic potion cited is **time.** When the theory of evolution is discussed, **time** is the panacea for all the thousands of problems that arise.

In nearly all discussions and debates about evolution that I have held at universities and colleges, I ask the evolutionists how certain things could have evolved by chance. Their answer is nearly always "Given enough time..." **Time** is the evolutionists' god. **Time** is able to accomplish anything the evolutionists can propose. **Time** can easily turn a frog into a prince. **Time** can create matter from nothing and life from matter. According to evolutionists, **time** can create order from chaos.

If **time** were to be removed from the above equation, the following three results would occur:

- The obvious impossibility of evolution would be clearly seen.
- Evolutionists would scream like a baby whose pacifier has been pulled out because they know that if time is removed, the silliness of their religion (evolution is religion, not science) will be exposed.
- Creation would become the only reasonable alternative explanation for the existence of this complex universe.

Just One Proof of a Young Earth Settles the Case Against Evolution

"This notion of species as 'natural kinds' fits splendidly with creationist tenets of a pre-Darwinian age. Louis Agassiz even argued that species are God's individual thoughts, made incarnate so that we might perceive both His majesty and His message. Species, Agassiz wrote, are 'instituted by the Divine Intelligence as the categories of his mode of thinking'. But how could a division of the organic world into discrete entities be justified by an evolutionary theory that proclaimed ceaseless change as the fundamental fact of nature?"
—**Stephen Jay Gould,** **Professor of Geology and Paleontology, Harvard University,"A Quahog is a Quahog," in "The Panda's Thumb: More Reflections in Natural History," [1980], Penguin: London, 1990, reprint, pp.170-171)**

Let's imagine we are exploring an old gold mine, and we find a Casio Databank watch half buried in the mud on the floor of the mine. Suppose, also, that the correct time and date are displayed on the watch and it is still running smoothly. Then imagine that I tell you the watch has been there for over **one thousand years.**

"That's impossible!" you say. "That watch could not have been there for a thousand years, and I can prove it!"

"How can you prove I'm wrong?" I say.

"Well, for one thing, this mine was dug just 150 years ago," you say.

"Okay," I admit, "you're right about the thousand years being too much, but the watch has been here for 150 years at least!"

"No!" you say. "Casio didn't make the Databank watch until twelve years ago."

"All right," I say. "The watch was dropped here twelve years ago then."

"Impossible!" you say. "The batteries only last five years on that watch, and it's still running. That proves it has been here less than five years."

While we still can't prove exactly when the watch was left there, you have logically limited the date to five years at the most. You have effectively proven my initial statement about 1000 years wrong. The larger numbers prove nothing in this debate. Even if I were to carbon date the mud or the plastic in the watch to try to prove that it is thousands of years old, my data would be meaningless. The same logic can be applied to finding the age of the earth. If several factors limit the age of the earth to a few thousand years, the earth cannot be older than a few thousand years! Even if a few indicators seem to show a greater age for the earth, it takes only ONE fact to prove the earth is young. We cover many points on this topic in seminar part #1 of the Seminar Series.

The Bible teaches that: God created the universe approximately 6000 years ago, ex nihilo (out of nothing) in six literal, twenty-four hour days. Then, approximately 4400 years ago, the earth was destroyed by a worldwide Flood. This devastating, year-long Flood was responsible for the sediment layers being deposited (the water was going and returning, Genesis 8:3-5). As the mountains rose and the oceans sank in after the Flood (Psalm 104:5-8, Genesis 8:1), the waters rushed off the rising mountains into the new ocean basins. This rapid-erosion through still-soft, unprotected sediments formed the topography we still see today in places like the Grand Canyon. The uniformitarian assumption—that today's slow erosion rates that take place through solid rock are the same as has always been—is faulty logic, and ignores catastrophes like the Flood. (2 Peter 3:3-8 says that the scoffers are "willingly ignorant" of the Flood.) See Seminar video #4 and #6 for more on this topic.

Sources

1 Morris, Henry M. *Scientific Creationism*. El Cajon, Calif.: Master Books, April 1985. Available from CSE ($9.50)

2 McLean, G. S.; McLean, Larry; Oakland, Roger. *The Bible Key to Understanding the Early Earth*. Oklahoma City, Okla.: Southwest Radio Church, 1987.

3 Huse, Scott M. *The Collapse of Evolution*. Grand Rapids, Mich.: Baker Book House, 1983.

4 Ackerman, Paul D. *It's a Young World After All*. Grand Rapids, Mich.: Baker Book House, 1986.

5 Blick, Edward F. *A Scientific Analysis of Genesis*. Oklahoma City, Okla.: Hearthstone Publ. Ltd., 1991.

6 Petersen, Dennis R. *Unlocking the Mysteries of Creation*. Available from CSE ($24.50)

7 Hovind, Kent E. *Creation Seminar, Parts 1-7* (most items referenced on screen—available from Creation Science Evangelism, 29 Cummings Road Pensacola, FL 32503).

8 Wysong, R. L. *The Creation-Evolution Controversy*. Midland, Mich.: Inquiry Press, 1976.

9 Baker, Sylvia. *Bone of Contention*. Creation Science Foundation Ltd., Sunnybank, Queensland 1990. Available from CSE ($3.50)

10 Moore, John N. *Questions and Answers on Creation-Evolution*. Grand Rapids, Mich.: Baker Book House, 1977.

11 Brown, Walt. *In the Beginning*. Center for Scientific Creation, 5612 North 20th Place, Phoenix, Ariz. Available from CSE ($23.50)

12 Morris, John D. *The Young Earth*. Master Books, 1994. Available from CSE ($14.50)

Listed below are some of the factors from various branches of science that limit the age of the universe or earth to within a few thousand years. Though it cannot be scientifically proven exactly when the universe was created, its age can be shown to NOT be billions of years. Each of the following evidences of a young earth is described in great detail in the books referred to in the side column. **Source number** and page number are given for the following statements:

Evidence from Space

1 The shrinking sun limits the earth-sun relationship to fewer than billions of years. The sun is losing both mass and diameter. Changing the mass would upset the fine gravitational balance that keeps the earth at just the right distance for life to survive. (**1**, p. 169; **2**, p. 30; **4**, pp. 56-63; **5**, p. 26; **6**, p. 43; **7**; **11**, p.34-35)

2 The ½ inch layer of cosmic dust on the moon indicates the moon has not been accumulating dust for billions of years. (**2**, p. 26; **3**, p. 22; **4**, p. 15; **6**, p. 35; **7**; **9**, p. 25; **11**, pp. 33, 80,) NOTE: Insufficient evidence to be positive

3 The existence of short-period comets indicates the universe is less than billions of years old. (**2**, p. 31; **3**, p. 27; **4**, p. 35; **6**, p. 37; **11**, p.29; **12**, p.22)

4 Fossil meteorites are very rare in layers other than the top layers of the earth. This indicates that the layers were not exposed for millions of years as is currently being taught in school textbooks. (**4**, p. 26; **11**, pp. 27, 67)

5 The moon is receding from the Earth a few inches each year. Billions of years ago the moon would have been so close that the tides would have been much higher, eroding the continents quickly. (**3**, p. 25; **6**, p. 43; **7**; **11**, p. 33)

6 The moon contains considerable quantities of U-236 and Th-230, both short-lived isotopes that would have been long gone if the moon were billions of years old. (**8**, p. 177; see also **4**, p. 51 & **11**, p. 28 for information on rock "flow")

7 The existence of great quantities of space dust, which by the Poynting-Robertson effect would have been vacuumed out of our solar system in a few thousand years, indicates the solar system is young. (**3**, p. 29; **6**, p.44; **11**, p. 33, 80; **12**, pp.87-88)

8 At the rate many star clusters are expanding, they could not have been traveling for billions of years. (**3**, p. 29; **4**, pp. 30 and 59; **6**, p. 44; **11**, p. 82)

9 Saturn's rings are still unstable, indicating they are not billions of years old. (**4**, p. 45; **7**, **11**, p.22-23)

10 Jupiter and Saturn are cooling off rather rapidly. They are losing heat twice as fast as they gain it from the sun. They cannot be billions of years old. (**5**, p. 26; **4**, p. 43;)

11 Jupiter's moon, Io, is losing matter to Jupiter. It cannot be billions of years old. (**4**, p. 3; **7,11**, p. 23)

12 Jupiter's moon, Ganymede has a strong magnetic field. (**7**)

"The Big Bang is presumed to have produced just hydrogen and helium, only 2 of the 92 elements of the earth's crust."
—**Dr. Robert V. Gentry,** Research Physicist

"As a matter of fact, however, it may be stated categorically that no archeological discovery has ever controverted a Biblical reference."
—**Nelson Glueck**, *Rivers in the Desert,* 1959, p. 31 Palestinian archeologist

"I myself am convinced that the **theory of evolution,** especially the extent to which it's been applied, will be one of the **great jokes** in the history books of the future. Posterity will marvel that so flimsy and dubious an hypothesis could be accepted with the incredible credulity that it has."
—**Malcolm Muggeridge,** journalist and philosopher, Pascal Lectures, University of Waterloo, Ontario, Canada

Among other factors to consider is that all the ancient astronomers from 2000 years ago recorded that Sirius was a red star—today it is a white dwarf. Obviously, the view of modern astronomy textbooks that billions of years are required for a star to 'evolve' from a red giant to a white dwarf needs to be restudied.(4, p.7)

Evidence from Earth

13 The decaying magnetic field limits earth's age to less than billions. (**1**, p. 157; **2**, p. 27; **3**, p. 20; **5**, p. 23; **6**, p. 42; **9**, p. 25; **10**, p. 38; **11**, p. 32, 80; **12**, p.91)

14 The volume of lava on earth divided by its rate of efflux gives a number of only a few million years, not billions. I believe that during the Flood, while "the fountains of the deep were broken up," most of the earth's lava was deposited rapidly. (**1**, p. 156; **11**, p.26)

15 Dividing the amount of various minerals in the ocean by their influx rate indicates only a few thousand years of accumulation. (**1**, p. 153; **5**, p. 24; **6**, p. 42; **11**, p. 26)

16 The amount of Helium 4 in the atmosphere, divided by the formation rate on earth, gives only 175,000 years. (God may have created the earth with some helium which would reduce the age more.) (**1**, p. 151; **6**, p. 42; **9**, p. 25; **11**, p. 25; **12**, 83-84)

17 The erosion rate of the continents is such that they would erode to sea level in less than 14,000,000 years, destroying all old fossils. (**2**, p. 31; **6**, p 38; American Science Vol 56 pp 356-374; **11**, p. 31, 79; **12**, pp. 88-90)

18 Topsoil formation rates indicate only a few thousand years of formation. (**6**, p. 38; **12**, p.94)

19 Niagara Falls' erosion rate (4 - 7 feet per year) indicates an age of less than 8400 years. Don't forget Noah's Flood could have eroded half of the seven and a half-mile-long Niagara River gorge in a few hours as the flood waters raced through the soft sediments.) (**6**, p. 39; **7**; **12**, pp.48-49)

20 The rock encasing oil deposits could not withstand the pressure for more than a few thousand years. (**2**, p. 32; **3**, p. 24; **5**, p. 24; **6**, p. 37; **7**; **11**, p. 26)

21 The size of the Mississippi River delta, divided by the rate mud is being deposited, gives an age of less than 30,000 years. (The Flood in Noah's day could have washed out 80% of the mud there in a few hours or days, so 4400 years is a reasonable age for the delta.) (**3**, p. 23; **6**, p. 38; **7**)

22 The slowing spin of the earth limits its age to less than the "billions of years" called for by the theory of evolution. (**3**, p. 25; **7**)

23 A relatively small amount of sediment is now on the ocean floor, indicating only a few thousand years of accumulation. This embarrassing fact is one of the reasons why the continental drift theory is vehemently defended by those who worship evolution. (**1**, p. 155; **6**, p. 28; **7**; **11**, p.31; **12**, p.90)

"Scientists who go about teaching that evolution is a fact of life are great con-men, and the story they are telling may be the greatest hoax ever. In explaining evolution, we do not have one iota of fact."
—**Dr. T. N. Tahmisian,** Atomic Energy Commission, USA

24 The largest stalactites and flowstone formations in the world could have easily formed in about 4400 years. (**5**, p. 27; **6,** p. 39; **7**)

25 The Sahara desert is expanding. It is about 4000 years old. See any earth science textbook. (**7**—Part 1B)

26 The oceans are getting saltier. If they were billions of years old, they would be much saltier than they are now. (**7**; **9**, p. 26; **10**, p. 37; **12**, p.85-87)

27 Ice accumulation at the poles indicates less than 5000 years (**7**)

Evidence from Biology

28 The current population of earth (6 billion souls) could easily be generated from eight people (survivors of the Flood) in less than 4000 years. (**1**, p. 167; **3,** p. 27; **6**, p. 41; **7;12**, p70-71)

29 The oldest living coral reef is less than 4200 years old.(**6**, p. 39; **7**)

30 The oldest living tree in the world is about 4300 years old. (**6**, p. 40; **7**)

Another factor to consider: The genetic load in man is increasing. Geneticists have cataloged nearly 1300 genetic disorders in the human race. It is certainly reasonable to believe that the human race was created perfect from the hand of the Creator but has been going downhill as a result of our disobedience to the laws established by the Creator. The Bible teaches that we live in a sin-cursed world as a result of Adam's sin.

Evidence from History

31 The oldest known historical records are less than 6000 years old. (**1**, p. 160)

32 Many ancient cultures have stories of an original creation and a worldwide Flood in the recent past. Nearly 300 of these flood legends are now known.(**7**) (See www.creationism.org)

33 Biblical dates add up to about 6000 years. (**7**)

"As yet we have not been able to trace the phylogenetic history of a single group of modern plants from its beginning to the present."
—**Chester A. Arnold**, Professor of Botany and Curator of Fossil Plants, University of Michigan in *An Introduction to Paleobotany,* P. 7

Those who believe the earth is billions of years old will typically try to discredit one or two of these evidences and then mistakenly think that they have successfully proven the entire list wrong. This is not logical, of course. Each evidence stands independently: it only takes one to prove the earth is young. The burden of proof is on the evolutionists if they expect all taxpayers to fund the teaching of their religion in the school system. Many who believe in evolution are great at "straining at a gnat, and swallowing a camel" (Mt. 23:24).

Evolutionists love to assume uniformitarian processes. Many of the preceding evidences follow the same logic evolutionists use all the time in dealing with carbon dating, strata formation, genetic drift, etc.

It is interesting to read the ramblings of nay-sayers like Scott, Matson, Babinski, etc. and see how many times they use words like: we believe, perhaps, could have, there is some reason to believe, etc. Evolutionists need billions of years to make people believe a rock can turn into a rocket scientist, but those years are not available.

"There is no doubt that natural selection is a mechanism, that it works. It has been repeatedly demonstrated by experiment. The question of whether it produces new species is quite another matter. No one has ever produced a species by mechanisms of natural selection. No one has ever gotten near it. And most of the current argument in neo-Darwinism is about this question: how a species originates and it is there that natural selection seems to be fading and chance mechanisms of one sort or another are being invoked."
—**Dr. Colin Patterson,** on the subject of Cladistics, in an interview with BBC, March 4, 1982. Dr. Patterson is Senior Paleontologist at the British Museum of Natural History, London, England.

"Still doubts about the sequence about man's emergence remain. Scientists concede that their most cherished theories are based on embarrassingly few fossil fragments and that huge gaps exist in the fossil record."
—**Time Magazine,** November 7, 1977

The following Bible verses tell when "the beginning" was:

- In **the beginning** God created the heaven and the earth. (Genesis 1:1)
- Moses because of the hardness of your hearts permitted you to put away your wives: but from **the beginning** it was not so. (Matthew 19:8)
- But from **the beginning** of the creation God made them male and female. (Mark 10:6)
- In **the beginning** was the Word, and the Word was with God and the Word was God. (John 1:1)
- That which was from **the beginning,** which we have seen with our eyes and our hands have handled, of the Word of life. (1 John 1:1)
- He that committeth sin is of the devil; for the devil sinneth **from the beginning**. (1 John 3:8)
- For then shall be great tribulation, such as was not since **the beginning** of the world to this time. (Matthew 24:21)
- Ye are of your father the devil.... He was a murderer from **the beginning**. (John 8:44)
- That the blood of all the prophets, which was shed from the **foundation of the world**, may be required of this generation; From the blood of Abel. (Luke 11:50, 51)
- And, Thou, Lord, in **the beginning** hast laid the foundation of the earth. (Hebrews 1:10)
- For in six days the **Lord made heaven and earth,** the sea, and all that in them is. (Exodus 20:11)
- The works were finished **from the foundation of the world.** For ... God did rest the seventh day from all his works. (Hebrews 4:3, 4)
- For in those days shall be affliction, such as was not from **the beginning of the creation** which God created unto this time. (Mark 13:19)
- Have ye not known? have ye not heard? hath it not been told you from **the beginning?** have ye not understood from the **foundations** of the earth? (Isaiah 40:21)
- Who hath wrought and done it, calling the generations from **the beginning?** I the Lord am He. (Isaiah 41:4)
- Have ye not read, that he which made them at **the beginning** made them male and female? (Matthew 19:4, Mark 10:6)
- For the invisible things of him from **the creation** of the world are clearly seen, being understood by the things that are made. (Romans 1:20)

Testing the Theory of Evolution

"The more statistically improbable a thing is, the less we can believe it happened by blind chance. Superficially the obvious alternative to chance is an intelligent Designer."
—**Dr. Richard Dawkins,** Department of Zoology, Oxford University, in "The Necessity of Darwinism," *New Scientist,* April 15, 1982, p. 130

"The [evolutionary] origin of birds is largely a matter of deduction. There is no fossil evidence of the stages through which the remarkable change from reptile to bird was achieved."
—**W. E. Swinton**, British Museum of Natural History, London, in *Biology and Comparative Physiology of Birds,* vol 1, p. 1

Alterations Needed to Change a Reptile into a Bird:

• A variety of feathers
• Growth of wings
• Strengthening of certain muscles
• Higher blood sugar levels and body temperature levels
• **Total** revision of respiratory, nervous, and reproductive systems.
• Lightening of bones
• New digestive system
• New "instinctive" behaviors

Questions for Evolutionists

The test of any theory is whether or not it provides answers to basic questions. Some well-meaning but misguided people think evolution is a reasonable theory to explain man's questions about the universe. Evolution is not a good theory—it is just a pagan religion masquerading as science. The following questions were distributed to the 750-plus people who attended my debate at Winona State University in Winona, Minnesota, on January 9, 1993. (The video-taped debate is #6 in my catalog, $9.95.) Questions added since the debate are marked with an asterisk (*).

• 1 Where did the space for the universe come from?
• 2 Where did matter come from?
• 3 Where did the laws of the universe come from (gravity, inertia, etc.)?
• 4 How did matter get so perfectly organized?
• 5 Where did the energy come from to do all the organizing?
• 6 When, where, why, and how did life come from non-living matter?
• 7 When, where, why, and how did life learn to reproduce itself?
• 8 With what did the first cell capable of sexual reproduction reproduce?
• 9 Why would any plant or animal want to reproduce more of its kind since this would only make more mouths to feed and decrease the chances of survival? (Does the individual have a drive to survive, or the species? How do you explain the origin of?)
• 10 How can mutations (recombining of the genetic code) create any new, improved varieties? (Recombining English letters will never produce Chinese books.)
• 11 Is it possible that similarities in design between different animals prove that they had a common designer instead of a common ancestor?
• 12 Natural selection only works with the genetic information available and tends only to keep a species stable. How would you explain the increasing complexity in the genetic code that must have occurred if evolution were true?
• 13 When, where, why, and how did
    a. single-celled plants become multi-celled?
    b. two and three-celled intermediates evolve?
    c. single-celled animals evolve?
    d. fish change to amphibians?
    e. amphibians change to reptiles?
    f. reptiles change to birds? (The lungs, bones, eyes, reproductive organs, heart, method of locomotion, body covering, etc., are all very different!)
    g. intermediate forms live?

> "In recent years several authors have written popular books on human origins which were based more on fantasy and subjectivity than on fact and objectivity. At the moment science cannot offer a full answer on the origin of humanity..."
> —**Dr. Robert Martin,** Senior Research Fellow, Zoological Fellow, Zoological Society of London

> "...There are gaps in the fossil graveyard, places where there should be intermediate forms, but where there is nothing whatsoever instead. No paleontologist writing in English (R. Carroll, 1988), French (J. Chaline, 1983), or German (V. Fahlbusch, 1983), denies that this is so. It is simply a fact. **Darwin's theory and the fossil record are in conflict.**"
> —David Berlinsky,
> *Commentary,* September 1996 p.28

> "As by this theory innumerable transitional forms must have existed, why do we not find them embedded in countless numbers in the crust of the earth? The number of intermediate links between all living and extinct species must have been inconceivably great!"
> —**Charles Darwin**

• 14 When, where, why, how, and from what did
  a. whales evolve?
  b. sea horses evolve?
  c. bats evolve?
  d. eyes evolve?
  e. ears evolve?
  f. Hair, skin, feathers, scales, nails, claws, etc., evolve?

• 15 Which evolved first (how, and how long, did it work without the others)?
  a. The digestive system, the food to be digested, the appetite, the ability to find and eat the food, the digestive juices, or the body's resistance to its own digestive juice (stomach, intestines, etc.)?
  b. The drive to reproduce or the ability to reproduce?
  c. The lungs, the mucus lining to protect them, the throat, or the perfect mixture of gases to be breathed into the lungs?
  d. DNA or RNA to carry the DNA message to cell parts?
  e. The termite or the flagellates in its intestines that actually digest the cellulose?
  f. The plants or the insects that live on and pollinate the plants?
  g. The bones, ligaments, tendons, blood supply, or muscles to move the bones?
  h. The nervous system, repair system, or hormone system?
  i. The immune system or the need for it?

• 16 There are many thousands of examples of symbiosis that defy an evolutionary explanation. Why must we teach students that evolution is the only explanation for these relationships?

• 17 How would evolution explain mimicry? Did the plants and animals develop mimicry by chance, by their intelligent choice, or by design?

• 18 When, where, why, and how did man evolve feelings? Love, mercy, guilt, etc. would never evolve in the theory of evolution.

• 19 *How did photosynthesis evolve?

• 20 * How did thought evolve?

• 21 *How did flowering plants evolve, and from what?

• 22 *What kind of evolutionist are you? Why are you not one of the other eight or ten kinds?

• 23 What would you have said seventy five years ago if I told you I had a living coelacanth in my aquarium?

• 24 *Is there one clear prediction of macroevolution that has proved true?

• 25 *What is so scientific about the idea of hydrogen gas becoming human?

• 26 *Do you honestly believe that everything came from nothing?

"One cannot be exposed to the law and order of the universe without concluding that there must be design and purpose behind it all.... To be forced to believe only one conclusion— that everything in the universe happened by chance—would violate the very objectivity of science itself.... They (evolutionists) challenge science to prove the existence of God. But must we really light a candle to see the sun? It is in scientific honesty that I endorse the presentation of alternative theories for the origin of the universe, life and man in the science classroom. It would be an error to overlook the possibility that the universe was planned rather than happening by chance."
—**Dr. Wernher von Braun**
(Father of American rocket and space program)

"We conclude — unexpectedly — that there is little evidence for the neo-Darwinian view: its theoretical foundations and the experimental evidence supporting it are weak."
—**Orr, H. A. & Coyne, J. A.,**
American Naturalist, 1992, p. 726

After you answer the previous questions, please look carefully at your answers and thoughtfully consider the following.

- 1 Are you sure your answers are reasonable, right, and scientifically provable, or do you just believe that it may have happened the way you have answered? (Do these answers reflect your religion or your science?)
- 2 Do your answers show more or less faith than the person who says, "God must have designed it"?
- 3 Is it possible that an unseen Creator designed this universe? If God is excluded at the beginning of the discussion by your definition of science, how could it be shown that He did create the universe if He did?
- 4 Is it wise and fair to present the theory of evolution to students as fact since over 90% of the population believe God created the universe?
- 5 What is the end result of a belief in evolution (lifestyle, society, attitude about others, eternal destiny, etc.)?
- 6 Do people accept evolution because of the following factors:
    a. It is all they have been taught?
    b. They like the freedom from God (no moral absolutes, etc.)?
    c. They are compelled to support the theory for fear of losing their job, peer status or grade point average?
    d. They are too proud to admit they are wrong?
    e. Evolution is the only philosophy that can be used to justify their political agenda?
- 7 Should we continue to use outdated, disproved, questionable, or inconclusive evidences to support the theory of evolution because we don't have a suitable substitute (Piltdown man, recapitulation, archaeopteryx, Lucy, Java man, Neanderthal man, horse evolution, vestigial organs, etc.)?
- 8 Should parents be allowed to require that evolution not be taught as fact in their school system unless equal time is given to other theories of origins (like divine creation)?
- 9 What are you risking if you are wrong? As one of my debate opponents said, "Either there is a God or there is not. Both possibilities are frightening."
- 10 Why are many evolutionists afraid of the idea of creationism being presented in public schools? If we are not supposed to teach religion in schools, then why not get evolution out of the textbooks? It is just a religious worldview.
- 11 Aren't you tired of faith in a system that cannot be true? Wouldn't it be great to know the God who made you, and to accept His love and forgiveness?
- 12 Would you be interested to see from the Bible how to have your sins forgiven and how to know for sure that you are going to Heaven? If so, call me.

The Evolution of Species by Means of Increasing Number of Chromosomes

-or-

The Preservation of Complex Life Forms in the Struggle for Life

-By Dr. Kent Hovind-

Number of Chromosomes:

Fern	480
White Ash	138
Carp	100
Goldfish	94
Sweet Potato	90
Turkey	82
Chicken	78
Dog	78
Duck	78
Horse	64
Cow	60
Silkworm	56
Cotton	52
Amoeba	50
Chimp	48
Tobacco	48
Human	46
Bat	44
Wheat	42
Soybean	40
Cat	38
Starfish	36
Apple	34
Alligator	32
Onion	32
Frog	26
Possum	22
Redwood	22
Kidney Bean	22
Corn	20
Marijuana	20
Carrot	20
Lettuce	18
Honeybee	16
Garden Pea	14
House Fly	12
Tomato	12
Fruit Fly	8
Penicillium	2

Possum, Redwood Tree, and Kidney Bean: "Our Ancestors"

A Spoof on Evolution Theory

The theory of evolution teaches that living things are becoming more complex as time progresses. Because the chromosomes in living matter are one of the most complex bits of matter in the known universe, it would seem logical to assume that organisms with the least number of chromosomes were the first ones to evolve and those with the most chromosomes are the end result of millions of years of evolution experimenting to increase complexity in living organisms. From the chart, it is "obvious" that we all started off as penicillium with only 2 chromosomes, and that we slowly evolved into fruit flies. After many millions of years we turned into tomatoes (or house flies) and so on, until we reached the human stage with 46 chromosomes. One of our ancestors must have been one of the identical triplets—possums, redwood trees, and kidney beans—with 22 chromosomes each.

If we are allowed to continue evolving we may someday be tobacco plants and maybe we may even become carp with 100, or maybe even the ultimate life form, a fern with **480** chromosomes!

Don't you believe it! God made this world and all life forms, as recorded in the Bible.

About the Great Flood and Noah's Ark

They, and every beast after his kind, and all the cattle after their kind, and every creeping thing that creepeth upon the earth after his kind, and every fowl after his kind, every bird of every sort. And they went in unto Noah into the ark, two and two of all flesh, wherein is the breath of life.
—**Genesis 7:14-15**

* See www.creationism.org for many flood legends.

A moon pool would provide:
1. Stress relief for a long ship
2. Air circulation
3. Place to dump refuse

Points to Ponder About Flood

2 Peter 3:3-8 tells us that people who scoff at the Bible are "willingly ignorant" of the Creation and the Flood. In order to understand science and the Bible, we must not be ignorant of those two great events in Earth's history.

- 1 Over 270 Flood legends* from all parts of the world have been found. Most have many similarities to the Genesis story.
- 2 Scoffers point out that 300-foot sailing ships leak. However, Noah's ark was built only to float, not to sail anywhere. Many ark scholars believe that the ark was a "barge" shape, not a pointed "boat" shape. This would greatly increase the cargo capacity.
- 3 Even using the small 18-inch cubit (my height is 6-ft. 1-in. and I have a 21-in. cubit) the ark was large enough to hold all the required animals, people, and food with room to spare.
- 4 The length-to-width ratio of 6 to 1 is what shipbuilders often use today. This is the best ratio for stability in stormy weather. (God thinks of everything!)
- 5 The ark may have had a "moon-pool" in the center. The larger ships would have a hole in the center of the bottom of the boat with walls extending up into the ship. There are several reasons for this feature:
  a. It allowed water to go up into the hole as the ship crested waves. This would be needed to relieve strain on longer ships.
  b. The rising and lowering water acted as a piston to pump fresh air in and out of the ship. This would prevent the buildup of dangerous gasses from all the animals on board and supply fresh air.
  c. The hole was a great place to dump garbage into the ocean without going outside.
- 6 The ark may have had large drogue (anchor) stones suspended over the sides to keep it more stable in rough weather. Many of these stones have been found in the region where the ark landed. See video #3 of our Seminar Series.
- 7 Noah lived 950 years! Many Bible scholars believe the pre-Flood people were much larger than modern man. Skeletons over 11 feet tall have been found! If Noah were taller, his cubit (elbow to fingertip) would have been much larger also. This would make the ark larger by the same ratio. See video #3 for more details.
- 8 God told Noah to bring two of each **kind** (seven of some), not of each **species** or variety. Noah had only two of the dog kind which would later became the wolves, coyotes, foxes, mutts, etc. The "kind" grouping is probably closer to our modern family division in taxonomy, and would greatly reduce the number of animals on the ark. Animals have diversified into many varieties in the last 4400 years since the Flood. This diversification is not anything similar to great claims that the evolutionists teach.

> And the ark rested in the seventh month... upon the mountains of Ararat.
> —**Genesis 8:4**

Mutations

- Humans are now subject to over 3500 mutational disorders.
- They are 1000 times more harmful than helpful.
- They don't create; they corrupt.
- They indicate creation (changes in genes that *already exist*).
- No one has ever observed mutations causing anything that could remotely resemble proof that any kind of plant or animal can or did change to another kind.

- 9 Noah did not have to get the animals. God brought them to him (Genesis 6:20, "shall come unto thee"). Also the pre-Flood world had more exposed land and less water. (See video #6)
- 10 Only land-dwelling, air-breathing animals with nostrils had to be included on the ark. (Genesis 7:15, 7:22 Noah did not need to take insects.)
- 11 Many animals sleep, hibernate, or become very inactive during bad weather or confinement and therefore consume less food.
- 12 All animals (and people) were vegetarians before and during the Flood according to Genesis 1:29-30 with Genesis 9:3.
- 13 The pre-Flood people were probably much smarter and more advanced than people today. The longer lifespans, Adam's pre-programmed mind and direct contact with God, and the fact that they could glean the wisdom of many generations that were still alive would greatly expand their knowledge base.
- 14 The Bible says that the highest mountains were covered by 15 cubits of water. This is half the height of the ark. The ark was safe from scraping bottom at all times. (Smart God!)
- 15 The large mountains, as we have them today, did not exist until after the Flood when the mountains arose and the valleys sank down (Psalms 104:5-9, Genesis 8:3-8).
- 16 There is enough water in the oceans right now to cover the earth 8,000 feet deep if the surface of the earth were smooth.
- 17 Many claim to have seen the ark in recent times in the area in which the Bible says it landed. There are two primary schools of thought about the actual site of the ark (see my Creation Seminar Part 3 video for more on this). Much energy and time has been expended to prove both views. Some believe the ark is on Mt. Ararat, covered by snow (CBS showed a one-hour special in 1993 about this site). The other group believes the ark is seventeen miles south of Mt. Ararat in a valley called "the valley of eight" (8 souls on the ark). The Bible says the ark landed in the "mountains" of Ararat, not necessarily on the mountain itself. (See www.wyattmuseum.com for this.)
- 18 The continents were not separated until 100-300 years after the Flood (Genesis 10:25). The people and animals had time to migrate anywhere on earth by then. (See video #6)
- 19 The top 3,000 feet of Mt. Everest (from 26,000-29,000 feet) is made up of sedimentary rock packed with seashells and other ocean-dwelling animals.
- 20 Sedimentary rock is found all over the world and formed in water.
- 21 Petrified clams in the closed position testify to their rapid burial while they were still alive.
- 22 Bent rock layers, fossil graveyards, oil, coal, and polystrate fossils are best explained by a Flood.
- 23 People choose to not believe in the Flood because it speaks of the judgment of God on sin (2 Peter 3:3-8).

The Blind Men and the Atheists (1990)

Two blind men argued
          into the night
About the great question:
          "Is there really sight?"
Said one to the other
          (and quite fervently),
"There cannot be colors
          or else we could see!
So take red and green
          and blue off the list.
If I cannot see them,
          they must not exist.

A crazy man told me
          the sky is bright blue.
I listened intently,
          but I caught no clue
Of anything out there
          to alter my mind.
I'm not deaf you know;
          I hear perfectly fine.
Be quiet and listen,
          and then you will know
That colors aren't real—
          How dare they say so!

They tell me that grass
          is some sort of green
It looks like the rest of
          the world that I've seen!
It tastes a lot different
          than jelly or cheese.
If I smell it too long,
          it sure makes me sneeze.
But to say that it's green?
          I'd have to say no
I will not believe it
          until I have seen.
There isn't a difference
          'twixt red, blue, or green!
And so the men argued
          with all of their might,

And I couldn't show them
          that they were not right.
They cannot see colors
          because they are blind!
So I couldn't get
          the truth in their minds.
Until they are given the great gift
          of sight,
Never, not ever will they "see the
          light."

Cont. next page

Battle Plan
Practical Steps to Fight Evolution

Many thinking people will agree that the theory of evolution is dangerous and should have no place in the classroom. What should we do to counter and combat this false teaching that is permeating and ruining our society via our tax-supported institutions?

Understand the Importance of the Conflict.

The theory of evolution, which is taught as a fact in our public school textbooks, tax-supported parks, museums, and public television programs, is actually not a harmless theory but a dangerous religious belief. I have dedicated my life to help people learn the truth needed to expose evolutionism as being largely responsible for molding the thinking of hosts of people like Adolph Hitler, Joseph Stalin, Pol Pot of the Khmer in Cambodia, Margaret Sanger, and Karl Marx, who have caused untold suffering in our world. Evolution as it is being taught is dangerous for several reasons. (See seminar part 5)

1 **At stake is the credibility of Jesus.** He cited Genesis twenty-five times and said the creation of Adam was "the beginning" (Matthew 19:4). Evolution and creation represent worldviews that are polar opposites—one of them is wrong! Also at stake are the morals of our children, because if evolution is true, there are no moral absolutes and only the strongest have a right to survive. If evolution is true, abortion, euthanasia, pornography, genocide, homosexuality, adultery, incest, etc., are all permissible.

2 **Evolution is positively anti-science.** Science deals with things that are testable, observable, and demonstrable, and evolution has none of those qualities. To call evolution "science" is to confuse fairy tales with facts. True, evolution has been mixed with science for the last 140 years, but that does not mean that it is the same as science. Beer is often advertised during sporting events but the two subjects have no logical connection, and evolution has no more to do with science than beer has to do with sports.

3 **Real science, not evolution, should be taught** in the science classes. Teaching the pagan religion of evolutionism is a waste of valuable class time and textbook space. It is also one of the reasons American kids don't test as well in science as kids in other parts of the world.

4 **Government should not sponsor religion.** Teaching the theory of evolution as fact in tax-supported schools violates the establishment clause of the First Amendment. Why should all taxpayers support one religion over all others in

Two atheists argued
    (on university sod)
About the great question,
    "Is there really a God?"
Said one to the other
    (and quite fervently),
"There can't be a God or
    else we could see.
So take that old Bible and
    God off the list.
If I cannot see Him,
    He must not exist.
Be quiet and listen,
    and then you will know,
That God is not real—
    how dare they say so!

A crazy man told me
    God lives up in Heaven
I used to believe that
    when I was just seven.
But now that I'm older
    and wiser, you see,
I will not believe it,
    you can't prove it to me.
I cannot sense God with
    sight, taste, or smell.
I do not believe in a
    Heaven or Hell!
I've never heard God
    or felt him at all;
If He's really up there,
    I wish He would call."

I said, "Listen fellows,
    you're spiritually blind.
You've only five
    entrances into your mind
That limits your input:
    I wish you could see,
You can't fathom God
    or eternity
There are lots of things
    that really are real.
It doesn't disprove God
    because you can't 'feel.'

So you two can argue
    the rest of the night.
There's no way to show you
    that you are not right.
When you get to Heaven
    (or Hell if you please)
You'll understand God
    and fall on your knees!
I wish you could see Him
    or hear Him somehow.
But that isn't possible
    where you are now.
To deny His existence
    is really absurd.
You'll have to believe Him
    and trust in His Word.

— Kent Hovind
    Written after the first
    debate with an evolutionist

our schools? Efforts must be made on all fronts to inform people that evolution is only a religion and that tax-supported institutions should not teach it as fact.

Live for God!

All our efforts to stem the tide of moral decay in our land are futile unless God leads and supports our cause. The most important thing anyone can do to help fix the problem is to obey 2 Chronicles 7:14 — "If my people, which are called by my name, shall humble themselves, and pray, and seek my face, and turn from their wicked ways; then will I hear from heaven, and will forgive their sin, and will heal their land."

1 **Pray for Wisdom.** Most importantly, ask God to give you wisdom (James 1:5) and direction about what He would have you do in His service. Jesus told us that we are to be the "salt of the earth." Salt preserves from corruption. One of our jobs is to preserve this world from corruption; if we do not preserve, we are worthless (see Matthew 5:13).

2 **Win Souls!** God called us to win souls, not causes. The great commission (Matthew 28:19-20; Mark 16:15, and Acts 1:8) commands us to preach, baptize, and teach people what Jesus taught His disciples. While there is nothing wrong with working for a cause (1 Samuel 17:29), Christians have a strong tendency to major on minors and minor on majors; we need to keep priorities in order. The battle raging for the minds of men is a battle between God and the Devil. The people who (knowingly or unknowingly) are working for the Devil are not the real enemy. There is a tendency among Christians to not keep the sin separate from the sinner. However, we can still use the advice given by Abraham Lincoln: "The best way to get rid of an enemy is to make him your friend." When dealing with evolutionists, our job is to love them and to keep a sweet spirit while trying to influence them to be saved. As we win people to Christ, they will begin to have their mind renewed and will see that God's Word is true. Our best offensive weapon is soul winning—converted evolutionists make great creationists! Most of the active creation scientists are former evolutionists. If we obey Christ and "preach the gospel to every creature," we will see great results.

To spread the Word, to edify the believers, or to evangelize the lost, order or copy extra sets of my tapes to loan, give as gifts, or donate to libraries at schools, churches, or even the public library. These tapes are regularly updated to improve quality and to add new research and artwork.

3 Don't Get Discouraged! "Be not weary in well doing" (2 Thessalonians 3:13). "Evil men and seducers shall wax worse and worse" (2 Timothy 3:13). "The battle is the Lord's" (1 Samuel 17:47). Our job is to be faithful until the Lord takes us out of this world. When the events of this world start to get you discouraged, read Psalm 2. The Devil may have his plans, but God in Heaven will laugh! Though I have worked for several years to get the textbooks changed, all that I have done so far is to keep the subject before the people. I have had no visible effect on the textbooks. It is our job to do right; God will take it from there.

Become Informed.

Often people are motivated to do something, but they don't have enough knowledge of the subject to be effective. Many good books have been written to help people learn the truth about creation and evolution. A list of some of these books is included in the annotated bibliography of this notebook. Also important is to become informed about the "New World Order" and the persecution that will come to Christians in America unless the Lord returns soon.

1 Know your rights. We need more Godly politicians, school board members, etc. to get involved in the political aspect of our great Republic while still possible. Students and parents involved in public schools need to know that they have many rights. Here are some good books on the subject which will be a great help to parents and students in learning what one can and cannot do for the Lord in his or her public school. (www.drdino.com/ Religious Freedoms)

Students' Legal Rights on a Public School Campus by J. W. Brinkley. Available from CSE ($9.50) or Roever Communications, P.O. Box 136130, Fort Worth, TX 76136, (817) 238-2005.

Students' Rights in the Public Education by John W. Whitehead. Available from CSE ($3.00) or from Rutherford Institute, P.O. Box 7482, Charlottesville, VA 22906-7482, (804) 978-3888.

Teaching Creation Science in Public Schools by Duane T. Gish. Available from CSE ($4.75) or from Institute for Creation Research, 10946 Woodside Avenue North, Santee, CA 92021 (619) 448-0900 www.icr.org

2 Call me for help. It is my privilege to travel and speak (more than 800 times each year) in public and private schools, university debates, churches, camps, and radio and television talk shows on the subjects of creation, evolution, and dinosaurs. It is my studied opinion that the Bible is the infallible, inspired, inerrant Word of the living God. The facts from science are clear; the entire universe was created by an all-wise Creator only a few thousand years ago. The original creation was perfect and very different than it is today. In the original creation, plants and animals

"Education is thus a most powerful ally of humanism. What can a theistic Sunday school's meeting for an hour once a week and teaching only a fraction of the children, do to stem the tide of the five-day program of humanistic teaching?"
—**Humanism: A New Religion,** 1930

"It may not be long before the practice of religion must be regarded as anti-science."
—**John Maddox,** editor of *Nature* (*American Spectator,* July, 1994)

Good News:
One-third of Americans read their Bible at least once a week.
Bad News:
54% can't name the authors of the four gospels.
63% don't know what a Gospel is.
58% can't name 5 of the 10 commandments.
10% Think Joan of Arc was Noah's wife.
New York Times, 12/7/97

"When [the devil] speaketh a lie, he speaketh of his own: for he is a liar, and the father of it."
—**John 8:44**

"No statute exists in any state to bar instruction in 'creation science.' It could be taught before, and it can be taught now."
—**Stephen Jay Gould** *The Verdict on Creationism,* New York Times July 19, 1987, p. 34

The word "Evolution" has many meanings, only one of which is scientific:
1. **Cosmic evolution**—the origin of time, space and matter; Big Bang.
2. **Chemical evolution**—the origin of higher elements from hydrogen.
3. **Stellar and planetary evolution**—origin of stars and planets.
4. **Organic evolution**—origin of life. Spontanious generation.
5. **Macroevolution**—changing from one kind of animal into another.
6. **Microevolution**—variations within kinds. Only this one has been observed and therefore qualifies as

lived longer and grew much bigger than they do currently (see Genesis 1:6-7; 5; 6:4, and my Creation Seminar videotape #2). In my seminars, I present many scientific evidences that the world is not "millions of years old." Most people are excited to learn that dinosaurs were in the Garden of Eden, have always lived with man, were on the ark with Noah, and a few may still be alive today in some parts of the world! (Creation Seminar videotape #3)

Students often call me for advice on how to handle various situations at school where they are being forced to learn things contrary to their beliefs on creation. Please feel free to call or write, if I can be of any help.

Please understand, when I talk about evolution I am not referring to simple variations that occur in any species. Dogs produce a variety of puppies, but never will dogs produce hamster or pine-tree offspring! Creationists do not argue that all dogs, wolves, and foxes may not have had a common ancestor, nor do they argue that natural selection does not occur. These would both be true whether plants and animals were created or evolved. However, real evolution, as presented in the textbooks, teaches that dogs share a common ancestor with pine trees! While anyone is certainly welcome to believe what he wants to believe, no intelligent person can say that evolution is real science, because evolution is not observable, testable, or demonstrable. My argument is not with science, but with evolution being improperly incorporated into science, where it has no place.

Influence your Area.

Everyone has a circle of people they can influence. At activities such as birthday parties, neighborhood Bible classes, Sunday school class parties, etc., you can show creation videos, have a creation speaker, or play games that teach the truth about dinosaurs and creation. You can also help private or home schools with your time, energy, and money. Come and visit Dinosaur Adventure Land for ideas.

Use the media (secular or Christian). A great way to reach people with the truth is to have your local radio or TV station contact me for an interview or call-in talk show on creation, evolution, dinosaurs, or the teaching in public schools. Secular stations are often glad to get such a controversial guest. I frequently do radio interviews by phone from my house and would be honored to appear on a program in your area. Local access cable TV stations are usually willing to air my videotapes.

"Let me control the textbooks, and I will control the state."
—**Adolf Hitler**

"The Supreme Court ruling did not, in any way, outlaw the teaching of 'creation science' in public school classrooms. Quite simply it ruled that, in the form taken by the Louisiana law, it is unconstitutional to demand equal time for this particular subject. 'Creation science' can still be brought into science classrooms if and when teachers and administrators feel that it is appropriate. Numerous surveys have shown that teachers and administrators favor just this route. And, in fact, 'creation science' is being taught in science courses throughout the country."

—Evolutionary biologist **Michael Zimmerman,** "Keep Guard Up After Evolution Victory," BioScience 37 (9, October 1987): 636

2 **Write letters to the editor.** Most local newspapers have a Letters to the Editor section. I have found this to be a great way to reach many people in an area, as each time I have written a letter to the editor, there has been a great response.

3 **Help teachers and school board members do right.** Most teachers, principals, board members, etc., involved in the public school system are sincere, dedicated professionals who want what is best for students. Often they face enormous pressure from small but vocal groups making them feel they are in the battle alone. Informed Christians can help by attending school board meetings, giving good creationist literature to these people and inviting them to creation lectures. Donate good books about creation science to your school's library. (FAQ for more details)

Learn the real (radical) agenda of the National Education Association (NEA), encourage public school teachers that you know to get out of the NEA and join alternative teachers unions.

Phyllis Schlafly (Eagle Forum), Alton, Illinois, (618) 462-5415 or eagle@eagleforum.org

Christian Educators Assn. Int., P.O. Box 41300, Pasadena, Cal. 91114, (626) 798-1124

Keystone Teacher's Association, P.O. Box 868, Mechanicsburg, Pa. 17055, (717) 432-1727

Concerned Educators Against Forced Unionism (CEAFU), 8001 Braddock Road, Springfield, Va. 22160, (703) 321-8519

4 **Review the textbook selections.** Of the fifty American states, twenty-two have a state textbook-selection committee, a group of people who look at the books available from all publishers for a given subject and then select five or six that they "approve." The list is then given to the local selection committee in each county. The county textbook selection committee will normally display the books for a few weeks, giving parents a chance to review them. After the committee decides which book to recommend, the school board votes to purchase that book for use in the county schools. Often the books are selected on a rotating basis, with a different subject being chosen each year. In the states without a state-level committee, each county, or district, or teacher may choose their own textbooks.

Any person in the county may review the books and make comments at the school board meeting. I would suggest that informed Christians in each county get involved in the selection process. The Gablers are fine Christian people and provide lots of information to help in the textbook selection process. The input of the Gablers in Texas will save lots of work for anyone wanting to get involved. Their organization reviews each new textbook as

Communist Rules for Revolution

1. Corrupt the young; get them away from religion.
2. Break down the old moral virtues.
3. Encourage civil disorders... and a soft government attitude toward crime.
4. Divide the people into hostile groups (race, religion, etc.).
5. Get the people's minds off their government by focusing their attention on athletics, sex, etc.
6. Get control of all media.
7. Destroy people's faith in their leaders.
8. Cause the registration of all firearms... To eventually confiscate them.

UNCENSORED

Communist Manifesto 1848

1. Abolition of private property
2. Heavy progressive income tax
3. Abolition of rights of inheritance
4. Confiscation of property rights
5. Central bank
6. Government ownership of communication and transportation
7. Government ownership of factories and agriculture
8. Government control of labor
9. Corporate farms, regional planning
10. Government control of education

it comes out, sending a copy of their review to anyone who requests it. The Gablers are fine Christian people and have worked on a donation basis for 40 years.

The Mel Gablers, Educational Research Analysts, P.O. Box 7518, Longview, Texas, 75607-7518, (903) 753-5993 www.textbookreviews.org

Which Books Are Better?

In 1991 a survey of textbooks was done to determine what percent of the book taught evolution. The results are below. Some books are more saturated with evolution than others.

Biology: An Everyday Experience	Merrill	2.9%
Focus on Life Science	Merrill	7.1%
Biology: Living Systems	Merrill	7.4%
Life Science	Scott, Foresman	8.5%
BSCS: An Ecological App. (Green version)	Kendall/Hunt	13.2%
BSCS: A Molecular App. (Blue version)	DC Heath	13.5%
Modern Biology	Holt, Rinehart	13.9%
Biological Science: An Inquiry into Life (Yellow Version)	Harcourt, Brace Javanovich	15.6%

Source: Impact #278, ICR P.O. Box 2667, El Cahon, CA 92021
See Icons of Evolution as well as Discovery Institute (www.crsc.org).

After you select a book for your school with the least amount of evolution, you should do several more things:

1. Write to the other textbook publishers and tell them why you did not select their books.
2. Write to the one you did select and tell them why you chose theirs.
3. Put a warning sticker in the front of the one you choose warning the students, by page number, of the false information it contains. See my video #4 or my booklet "Are You Being Brainwashed by Your Science Textbook?" for help on this. Demand that lies be removed from textbooks. About fifty lies are used to make students believe in evolution. Do not mention creation or evolution, just demand that books be factual. See seminar #4 for lots more on this topic.

Two Worldviews

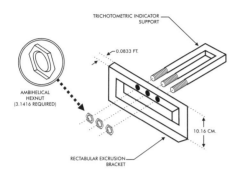

TRICHOTOMETRIC INDICATOR SUPPORT

0.0833 FT.

AMBIHELICAL HEXNUT (3.1416 REQUIRED)

10.16 CM.

RECTABULAR EXCRUSION BRACKET

Sometimes a first glance does not reveal crucial details.

Sci-ence n. [<Scire, to know] 1. Systematized knowledge derived from observation, study, etc. —Webster's Dictionary.

There are four great questions that man tries to answer in life. These are called the great philosophical questions. **Who am I? Where did I come from? Why am I here? Where am I going when I die?** The way you answer them depends upon your world view—the way you view the world.

There are two ways to look at the world. Some people look at the world and say, "You know, it's amazing, a big bang made this world from nothing!" This view is the humanist worldview, which says man is God. Humanism is the philosophy from which the idea of evolution comes, believing that there is no Creator—no God.

The second way to view the world is that since there is incredible design, there must have been a designer. This is the creationist worldview which says God is God: man is not God. These two worldviews are absolutely at war with each other.

How do we answer the four great questions of life? If evolution is true, we are nothing important. Actually, we are a bit of protoplasm that washed up on a beach after a Big Bang about 20 billion years ago. There is no purpose in life; so we might as well have fun. If it feels good—do it. After all, we are just going to end up in a grave to get recycled into a worm or a plant.

But the Bible says, "In the beginning God created the heaven and the earth." If that is true, we have a whole different set of answers to those four questions. God's creation of the world means that we had better find out who He is and what He wants. We were created in His image with a responsibility to obey Him. When we die, our choice in life will determine where we will spend eternity—in hell, separated from God, or in heaven with Him.

	Humanist View	Creationist View
Science (ex. Grand Canyon)	The Colorado River created the Grand Canyon over millions of years.	The Worldwide Flood created the Grand Canyon quickly as the waters receded.
Politics and Government	Democracy: 1. Laws come from man's opinion, 2. Rights are granted by government, 3. Government should be all-powerful provider.	Constitutional Republic: 1. Laws come from Creator, 2. Rights are "unalienable," 3. Government should be limited to the punishment of evil doers and defense.
Health	The body is a random collection of chemicals that formed by chance over millions of years. Diseases should be treated with drugs—**Drug Therapy.**	The body was designed by an all-wise Creator. He designed the food supply to provide our needs—**Nutrition Therapy.**

Physics

The First Law of Thermodynamics

The First Law of Thermodynamics states that matter and energy can neither be created nor destroyed although they may be converted from one form to another. This natural process can be seen in the world around us. Ice melting is one example of matter changing from one form to another, a solid into a liquid. The ice may change physical properties, but the mass before the reaction remains constant with the mass after the reaction. This law supports the Biblical view of creation, requiring a special miracle from God to account for all the matter and energy in the universe. Evolution attempts to credit the Big Bang with this miracle while denying that it violates the most basic law of the universe—**something cannot come from nothing.**

The Second Law of Thermodynamics

The Second Law of Thermodynamics simply states that everything tends toward disorder. If a truck carrying a stack of bricks hits a bump in the road causing the bricks to fall off, the bricks would not fall in their previously ordered state. They would fall randomly; and entropy would increase, illustrating the Second Law of Thermodynamics. The Bible describes the Second Law as extending from the earth to the heavens in Psalm 102:25-26, Isaiah 51:6, and Hebrews 1:10-11. Evolutionists contrive silly excuses and reasons to ignore this fundamental law of physics because it contradicts their pet theory.

Everything we observe in the universe verifies the laws of thermodynamics. The universe is wearing down, not winding up.

Evolutionists assume that adding energy (open system) will overcome the 2nd law of thermodynamics.
1. The universe is closed system
2. Adding energy is destructive without a complex mechanism to harness the energy.

The Japanese added lots of energy to Pearl Harbor in 1941 and did not organize any thing.

The sun's energy will destroy a roof, house, paint job...

Only a very complex molecule called chlorophyll can harness the sun's energy. One leaf cell is more complex than a city.

The evolutionist's "open system" excuse to believe the Second Law of Thermodynamics does not apply to Earth is silly.

The Law of Conservation of Angular Momentum

The Big Bang is A Big Dud.

"The ultimate origin of the solar system's angular momentum remains obscure."
—Well-known solar-system Evolutionist scientist, Dr. Stuart Ross Taylor, Solar System Evolution: A New Perspective, Cambridge University Press, p. 53, 1992.

Venus, Uranus and possibly Pluto rotate backwards from the other six planets.

I have little hesitation in saying that a sickly pall now hangs over the big bang theory."
— Sir Fred Hoyle, astronomer, cosmologist, and mathematician, Cambridge Univrsity. "The Big Bang Theory Under Attack". Science Digest, Vol. 92 May 1984, p. 84

Eight of the 91 moons rotate backwards. Jupiter, Saturn and Neptune have moons orbiting in both directions.
—Astronomical Almanac for the year 1989 (Wash. DC U.S. Government Printing Office, 1989) p. E88

The Law of Conservation of Angular Momentum describes the tendency of a spinning object to continue spinning in the same direction. Just as something traveling along a path tends to stay moving in that direction (linear momentum), the same is true for a spinning object—it continues to spin in the same direction. As an example, children riding on a merry-go-round, have angular momentum. Given sufficient speed, a child that jumps from the merry-go-round will travel in a straight line but will be spinning in the same direction as the merry-go-round. This scientific law contradicts the Big Bang Theory which proposes that a spinning cosmic explosion started the universe into its evolutionary process. If the Big Bang were true, all the planets should be spinning in the same direction today.

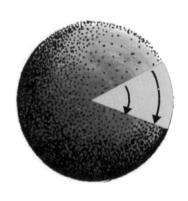

"This (Angular Momentum) would have caused the sun to spin very rapidly. Actually, our sun spins very slowly, while the planets move very rapidly around the sun. In fact, although the sun has over 99% of the mass of the solar system, it has only 2% of the angular momentum. This pattern is directly opposite to the pattern predicted for the nebular hypothesis."

—Dr. H. Reeves The Origin of the Solar System, Dermott, S.F. Ed. John Wiley & Sons, New York p. 9, 1978.

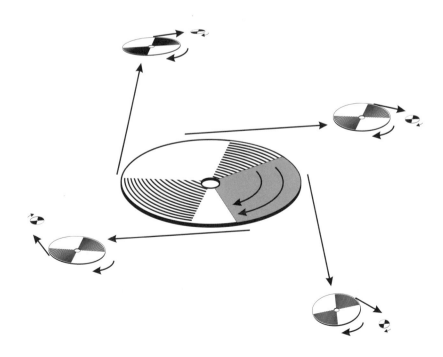

Evidence for a Young Universe

Egyptian hieroglyphs from 2000 B.C. described Sirius as red.
Cicero, in 50 B.C., Stated Sirius was red.
Seneca described Sirius as being redder than Mars.
Ptolemy listed Sirius as one of the six red stars in 150 A.D.
Today it is a white star-binary.
Textbooks say it should take billions of years for this to happen.
—*It's a Young World,* Paul Ackerman

"In the beginning, God created the heaven and the earth."
—Genesis 1:1

Galaxies

If spiral galaxies were billions of years old, the arms extending from their centers would have completely closed, causing the galaxies to lose their unique, spiral shape.

Red Giants

Evolutionists teach that red giant stars change into white dwarf stars over millions of years; yet Sirius is an example of a red star becoming white within the past 2,000 years. Ancient astronomers recorded that Sirius glowed red in the sky, yet now it is categorized as white. Obviously, the evolutionists' opinions of the length of time to change a red giant star into a white dwarf star are incorrect.

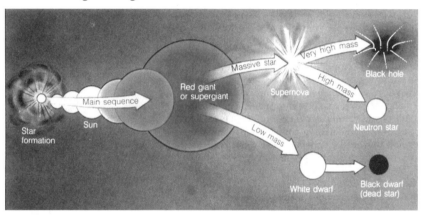

Jupiter and Saturn

These two planets radiate more heat than they receive from the sun. If they were billions of years old, both planets would have reached equilibrium and no longer be able to lose more heat than they receive.

Moon and Tides

The earth and the moon are inextricably linked via their mutual gravitational pull. The moon's primary effect on the earth is that of tides. These twice-daily tides inflict a barely perceptible drag on the earth's rotation, causing the earth's natural day to lengthen and the moon's orbit to recede. Because both gravitational forces and friction loss can be computed and predicted mathematically, we can determine how close the moon could orbit before resulting in lunar destruction or eradication of life on earth. With this in mind, the earth/moon relationship could not possibly be more than 1.2 billion years old, and geologic evidence indicates that it is much younger.

The heavens declare the glory of God and the firmament showeth his handy-work.
—Psalm 19:1

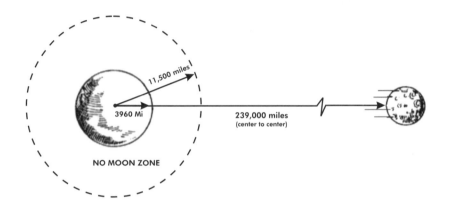

Comets

Composed of frozen gasses and small rocks, comets lose material when their orbit takes them close to the sun. The vapor produced gives the appearance of a tail, often the recognizable feature of a comet. A comet's life is relatively short, falling between an estimated 100 to 200 orbits around the sun. The frequency of comets has consistently decreased through the years, alluding to a much younger universe than textbooks describe.

Humanists regard the Universe* as self existing and not created.
—Humanists Manifesto 1 (1933) Tenent #1

*Notify the capital "U" to deify universe.

Uni = single
Verse = spoken sentence

And God said, "Let there be..."
—Genesis 1:3

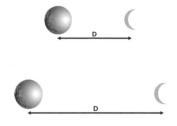

*Inverse Square Law—The principle in which intensity, such as gravitational pull, and distance are directly proportional to each other. For example, if the distance is divided in half, the attraction is quadrupled (4 times).

$$\text{Intensity} = I/d^2$$

Evidence for a Young Earth

"Or speak to the earth, and it shall teach thee: and the fishes of the sea shall declare unto thee. Who knoweth not in all these that the hand of the LORD hath wrought this?"
—Job 12:8-9

The Oldest Tree:

A **Bristle cone pine** is approximately 4,300 years old—dated via tree rings. The method may not be perfect, but it is the best we have for dating trees.

The Oldest Reef:

The **Great Barrier Reef** is less than 4,200 years old—dated via measuring the growth rate for 20 years. (Must have been a government job!)

Even though both are less than 5,000 years old, they are the two oldest-living organisms on earth. Their ages easily fit the creationist point of view, but leave loose ends for the evolutionist. Why aren't there older trees or bigger reefs? With the evolutionist timeline, surely something is closer in age to their "millions of years."

Evolution doesn't fit the facts, does it?

Earth's Slowing Rotation

"By what way is the light parted, which scattereth the east wind upon the earth?"
—Job 38:24

Prevailing winds are caused by two phenomena. The sun's heat causes north-south or south-north winds, depending on latitude. The rotation of the earth causes the winds to shift east or west—clockwise north of the equator and counterclockwise to the south. This **Coriolis Effect** is proportional to the speed of the earth's rotation: the greater the rotational speed, the greater the Coriolis

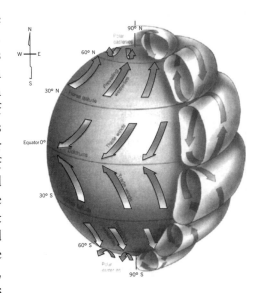

Effect. Due to these prevailing winds, the Sahara Desert is in the process of desertification, expanding approximately four miles per year. Calculations based upon the rate of the Sahara's expansion show the desert to be 4,000 years old. This young age of the Sahara Desert fits quite well in the creationist timeline, beginning its desertification process soon after the global flood. The current slowing rate of the earth's rotation, and its relationship with the

"People are the cause of all the problems; we need to get rid of some of them..."
—**Charles Wurster, Environmental Defense Fund.**

"The world has cancer, and the cancer is man."
—**Alan Gregg, Mankind at the Turning Point**, 1974.

Regardless of the future, the current population shows only 4400 years of growth.

The world is NOT overcrowded! Jacksonville, Florida has 25 billion square feet inside the city limits. Enough to hold all 6 billion people on the Earth today.

If it is overcrowded where you are:

MOVE!

Earth's magnetic strength has declined 6% in the last 150 years.
—**Astronomy and the Bible Donald DeYoung**, p. 18

Coriolis Effect, allows for a variety of climates around the world without creating a menacing environment. Following the evolutionist timeline over a period of millions of years, the Sahara Desert should have already expanded to its maximum size. However, since the earth's rotational speed is decreasing measurably, the Coriolis Effect would have been far greater millions of years ago, exacerbating the evolutionists' difficulty explaining the Sahara Desert's young age.

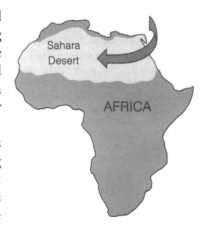

Population

In 1810, a billion people lived on earth. In less than 200 years, the population hit six billion. This fits the Biblical chronology perfectly as the current population started about 4,400 years ago with Noah and his family after the flood. An evolutionary timeline would require not only a nearly non-existent growth rate but also three trillion deceased humans within the last million years.*

* Dr. Henry Morris, Scientific Creationism, Masterbooks, Green Forest, AR, 1985, pp.167-169. Available from CSE ($9.50).

Declining Magnetic Field

Studies over the past 140 years show a consistent decay rate in the earth's magnetic field. At this rate, in as few as 25,000 years ago, the earth would have been unable to support life because of the heat from the electric current.

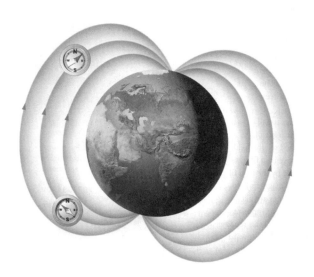

Fast Eroding Niagara Falls

"A gorge about 7 1/2 miles long runs just below Niagara Falls. A simple calculation shows that it has been 9900 years..."
—**Holt Earth Science**, 1984, p. 384
See also: In the Minds of Men, by Ian Taylor, p. 83, available from CSE.
See also Creation Ex Nihilo Sept-Nov, 2000 p. 8

After Charles Lyell published his Principles of Geology in 1830s, society began accepting the theory that the earth and mankind evolved from a previous lesser state. Lyell used Niagara Falls as one of his illustrations to promote uniformitarianism. He estimated that Niagara Falls was 10,000 years old. He did this to try to discredit the Bible. Skeptics like Lyell leave out one important factor in their calculations-a worldwide flood, approximately 4,400 years ago.

Factoring a worldwide flood into the equation, scientists arrive at a higher initial erosion rate for the 7 ½ mils Niagara Gorge. Since an increase in the quantity of water is directly related to the rate of erosion, the great volume of water receding after the flood could easily account for half of the erosion of Niagara Falls. Using the evolutionist time frame, Niagara Falls should have already eroded back into Lake Erie. The reason why Niagara Falls has not eroded farther over the "millions of years" of the earth's existence continues to elude evolutionists.

Science always seems to correspond with the creation timeline while evolutionists struggle to make their assumptions and theories plausible.

Salt in the Oceans

The water in the oceans contains 3.6% dissolved minerals, giving the ocean its salinity. Salt, composed of the elements sodium and chlorine, is the primary mineral. For years, scientists have been measuring the amount

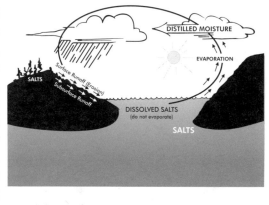

of sodium in the oceans and have found that an estimated 457 million tons are deposited into the oceans annually, while only 122 million tons leave the ocean via numerous methods.

Given the current amount of salt in the oceans, the data strongly favors a recent creation and global flood. If applied to the evolutionist's timeframe of millions of years, the oceans would be saturated by salt. Even using liberal estimates of salinity levels, the maximum possible age is 62 million years.

"It has been long felt that the average climate of the earth through time has been milder and more homogeneous than it is today. If so, the present certainly is *not* a very good key to the past in terms of climate."

—**Robert H. Dott and Roger L. Batten**, *Evolution of the Earth* (New York: McGraw-Hill, 1971), p. 298.

Just because Mr. Spark's religion (of evolution) happens to be included in this generation's science textbooks does not mean it qualifies as science or that it becomes science by association.

"In Greenland and Antarctica, where the weather is consistently dry and very cold, the glaciers are miles thick but the annual rings are very thin.

The deepest cores can measure over 10,000 feet, cores from Greenland drilled since 1990 show the northern climate was erratic... 135,000 years ago."

The Evolutioner

"Ice Core Proves Old Earth"

Denver, Col.—It's official: A startling new study by researchers from the National Ice Core Laboratory (NICL) confirm what evolutionists have been claiming for years—the earth is thousands of years old at the least! After an extensive study of a 10,000-foot ice core, a spokesperson announced that samples taken from Greenland contain 135,000 consecutive annual rings, or layers. These winter/summer sequences prove that the earth is much older than the 6,000 years Creationists believe.

The Truthful Times

Sunday, August 9, 1992

"Layers Not Annual"

Greenland—Ice core analysis was proven invalid with the completed excavation of *Glacier Girl*, one of the fighter planes that crash landed in Greenland during WWII. Discovered under 263 feet of ice and snow after only 42 years, the WWII aircraft clearly invalidated analysts' proposal that ice core layers result from annual weather variations.

Dr. Larry Vardiman stated, "…the ice sheet [above the aircraft] has been accumulating at an average rate of five feet per year." With approximately five feet of ice layers forming each year, scientists have found that <u>mild</u> weather variations cause ice layering, not just dramatic annual weather changes of summer and winter.

"The Greenland ice sheet averages almost 4000 feet thick," Dr. Vardiman explained. "If we were to assume the ice sheet has been accumulating at this rate since the beginning, it would take less than 1000 years for it to form and the recent-creation model might seem to be vindicated."

Larry Vardiman, Ph.D., "Ice Cores and the Age of the Earth,"
Vital Articles on Science/Creation, April 1992

Strata and Their Age

Q: I've never understood polystrate fossils. Aren't they evidence of evolution with all the different layers of strata they go through?

—M.L., South Carolina

A: Since the proposal of the idea of uniformity by Charles Lyell in the early 1800s, geologists have struggled to explain polystrate fossils. A polystrate fossil is a fossil encased not in a single layer of strata but in multiple layers. Uniformity, advocating that the "present is the key to the past," describes each layer being laid down over extensive periods of time. The problem with each layer taking so long to form is that most fossils found in these layers would have decayed prior to the forming of the next layer. Some examples that confirm the idea of rapid fossilization are as follows:

1. Fossil of ichthyosaur, buried and fossilized while giving birth (Creation Magazine, Dec. 99),

2. Petrified trees are found in scores of places around the world. See seminar part 4.

3. Polystrate trees found in France upside down extending through many layers (Bone of Contention by Silvia Baker, p. 12).

Polystrate fossils are found extending through multiple layers of sediment. Many trees have been found fossilized in a vertical position through layers of coal, sandstone, and other sediments. Certainly, the trees would have decayed if millions of years had occurred between the different strata.

Geologists fail to accept that the only reasonable explanation of polystrate fossils is that the layers formed quickly around plant and animal life before they had time to decay. Seems to correspond with the Biblical account of the worldwide flood, doesn't it?

See the Creation Seminar Series parts 4 and 6 for more information and pictures on this topic. Visit www.drdino.com for more pictures of

"The hurricane, the flood or the tsunami may do more in an hour or a day than the ordinary processes of nature have achieved in a thousand years. Given all the millennia we have to play with in the stratigraphical record, we can expect our periodic catastrophes to do all the work we want of them."

—**Derek V. Ager**, *The Nature of Stratigraphical Record* (New York: John Wiley & Sons, 1993), p.80.

Polystrate fossils such as this one are found all over the world. They run through many rock layers proving the rock layers are not different ages as the textbooks teach.

Rapid Cave Formation

Although most people believe that cave formations need millions of years to develop, stalactites and stalagmites grow rather quickly. Stalactites, recognized because they "stick tight" to the ceiling of most limestone caves, are deposits of calcium carbonate formed by the dripping of mineralized solutions. As the mineral deposits build up on the cave floor, stalagmites are formed. Occasionally, the connecting of the two will create a column extending from floor to ceiling.

The monitoring of many stalactites and stalagmites within the last century has shown the rate of growth to be much faster than the rate taught in many textbooks. Stalactites over five feet long have been found in the basement of the Lincoln Memorial, built in 1923, as well as some more than a foot long under bridges in Philadelphia, Pennsylvania.

Stalagmites grow somewhat slower that stalactites ; but they still do not take thousands of years to form. In 1953, Mason Sutherland published a photograph in National Geographic of a bat that had fallen on a stalagmite in the Carlsbad Caverns, New Mexico. The bat was covered and preserved before it could decompose, proving the rapid growth rate of some stalagmites.

Much more evidence exists for fast-growing stalactites and stalagmites (see video #1), yet textbooks and national parks continue to teach that they take countless thousands of years to form. Using a rapid growth rate, these cave formations could easily fit the Biblical timeline after the worldwide flood 4,400 years ago. Unfortunately, evolutionary scientists struggle to keep the Biblical timeline out of science although science, time after time, falls right into step with it.

> "In other words, it's natural selection or a Creator. There is no middle ground. This is why prominent Darwinists like G.G. Simpson and Stephen Jay Gould, who are not secretive about their hostility to religion, cling so vehemently to natural selection. To do otherwise would be to admit the probability that there is design in nature-and hence a Designer."
>
> —**George Sim Johnston**, "The Genesis Controversy," *Crisis* (May 1989), p. 17.

Rapid Fossilization

Although evolutionists have repeatedly presented fossils as evidence for an earth millions of years old, creationists, using the same fossils and an opposing interpretation, conclude they are evidence for a young earth. As the remains of plants and animals are covered by sediment, fossils are created. The compressed remains are preserved and converted into minerals, leaving an imprint in stone. In order for an organism to be fossilized, the remains must be covered quickly; otherwise, the natural decaying process begins.

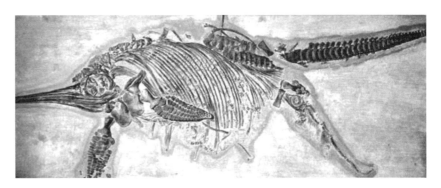

"Deposits of recent mud flows on Mount St. Helens demonstrate conclusively that stumps can be transported and deposited upright. These observations support the conclusions that some vertical trees in the Yellowstone 'fossil forests' were transported in a geologic situation directly comparable to that of Mount St. Helens."

—**William J. Fritz**, "Stumps Transported and Deposited Upright by Mount St. Helens Mud Flows," *Geology*, vol. 8 (December 1980), p. 588.

Evolutionists believe the principle of uniformity, implying that small changes over extended periods of time brought about significant changes. They have long used fossils to argue for their supposed old age of the earth's strata. However, fossils form quickly under special conditions involving rapid, immediate burial in mud just like Noah's flood would have provided.

Rapid fossilization, promoted by Biblical creation, easily explains the existence of fossils. Because of local flooding and volcanic activity around the world, not every fossil can be dated back to Noah's day. However, there are many fossils, such as polystrate fossils, that can only be explained by a worldwide flood. As the waters were "going and returning" (Genesis 8), great amounts of sediment began to settle into layers. This event allowed ample time for the remains of many plants, animals, and humans to be buried quickly and fossilized. Rapid fossilization scientifically answers the questions as to how fossils are formed; and theories made to the contrary will always leave more questions than answers.

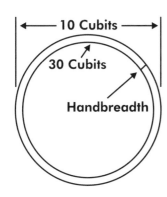

"And he made a molten sea, ten cubits from the one brim to the other: it was round all about, and his height was five cubits: and a line of thirty cubits did compass it round about.

And under the brim of it round about there were knops compassing it, ten in a cubit, compassing the sea round about: the knops were cast in two rows, when it was cast.

It stood upon twelve oxen, three looking toward the north, and three looking toward the west, and three looking toward the south, and three looking toward the east: and the sea was set above upon them, and all their hinder parts were inward.

And it was an hand breadth thick, and the brim thereof was wrought like the brim of a cup, with flowers of lilies: it contained two thousand baths."

— I Kings 7:23-26

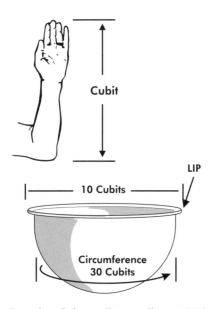

The Bible and the Value of π

Does the Bible contain a mathematical error?

I Kings 7:23–26 and II Chronicles 4:2–5 describe a huge brass bowl (sea) built by King Solomon. If the diameter of this bowl was 10 cubits, then the circumference should have been 31.415926...cubits, not just 30 cubits! Any math student will tell you that the circumference of a circle is found by taking the diameter times Pi (π). This apparent mathematical error caused me, as a new Christian, to doubt the accuracy of the Bible.

The answer is so simple!

The diameter of 10 cubits is from outer rim to outer rim, the way anyone would measure a circular object. The circumference of 30 cubits, however, was of the inner circle, after subtracting the thickness of the brass (two handbreadths—one for each side) from which the bowl was made. This would be the number needed to calculate the volume of water.

Check for yourself.

Substitute the length of your cubit (elbow to longest fingertip) for the letter C in the following formula, and solve for H (handbreadth).

$$30C \div \pi + 2H = 10C$$

The width of your handbreadth will be the result. For example, my cubit is 20 inches long. If I had built the brass bowl, the inner diameter would have a circumference of 600 inches (30 x 20 inches) and a diameter of 190.986 inches (600 inches ÷ 3.14159). The difference between the two diameters is 9.014 inches (two of my handbreadths).

Rest assured.

God makes no mistakes, mathematical or otherwise. The Scriptures do not contain error. By the way, Solomon built this sea in 1000 B.C., long before the Greeks rediscovered Pi (π). We may not understand some things at first glance, but the problem is with us, not with the Bible. Please be sure you are on the solid foundation of God's Word, saved by the blood of Christ.

A second way to solve this supposed contradiction has also been proposed. Since the Bible says the sea had a lip like the brim of a cup, the ten cubit measurement may have included the lip while the circumference be around the bowl without the lip.

Contradictions in the Bible?

Do Genesis chapters 1 and 2 conflict? Many scoffers claim that the Bible is full of contradictions. They will nearly always cite Genesis 1 and 2 as examples.

1. Genesis 1:11 has the trees made on day 3 before man; Genesis 2:8 has the trees made on day 6 after man.
2. Genesis 1:20 has birds made out of the water on day 5; Genesis 2:19 has birds made out of the ground (after man) on day 6.
3. Genesis 1:24, 25 has the animals made on day 6 before man; Genesis 2:19 has the animals made on day 6 after man.

Here is the solution.

A careful reading of the two chapters will show the solution for each of the supposed contradictions.

Explanation of supposed contradiction 1:

a. Chapter 1 tells the entire story in the order it happened.

b. Genesis 2:4–6 gives a quick summary of the first five days of creation.

c. Genesis 2:7–25 is describing only the events that took place on day 6 in the Garden of Eden.

d. The trees described in Genesis 2:8 are only in the Garden (the rest of the world is already full of trees from day 3). The purpose of this second creation of trees may have been to let Adam see that God did have power to create, that He was not just taking credit for the existing world. Notice that the second creation of trees was still on day 6 and was only those trees that are "pleasant to the sight and good for food."

Explanation of supposed contradiction 2:

The birds created out of the ground on day 6 are only one of each "kind" so that Adam can name them and select a wife. The rest of the world is full of birds from day 5.

Explanation of supposed contradiction 3:

Genesis 2:19 is describing only the animals created in the Garden, after man. The purpose of this second batch of animals being created was so that Adam could name them (Genesis 2:19) and select a wife (Genesis 2:20). Adam did not find a suitable one (God knew he wouldn't), so God made Eve (Genesis 2:21–22).

There are no contradictions between these two chapters. Chapter 2 only describes in more detail the events in the Garden of Eden on day 6. If ancient man had written the Bible (as some scoffers say), he would never have made it say that the light was made before the sun! Many ancient cultures worshiped the sun as the source of life. God is light. God made the light before He made the sun so we could see that He (not the sun) is the source of life.

Folks, the only contradictions in the Bible are **APPARENT** contradictions. Many are dealt with on the video #7 and on the web site www.drdino.com.

If God had made Adam last, Satan could claim that he created it all. Adam would not have seen God do it. Eve was made last and did not see God create anything. She was the one Satan deceived.

Of Governments and Cows

How Types of Governments View Property Rights

"Every effort has been made by the Federal Reserve Board to conceal its powers, but the truth is...the Fed (Federal Reserve System) has usurped the government. It controls everything here (Congress) and it controls all our foreign relations. It makes and breaks governments at will."
—Louis T. McFadden (murdered), ex-Chairman, House Committee on Banking and Currency

"The surest way to destroy a nation is to debauch its currency."
—Vladimir Lenin

"Permit me to issue and control a nation's money, and I care not who makes its laws"
—Mayer Amschel Rothschild

Biblical Capitalism: You have two cows. You take care of them and sell the extra milk if you want to.

Feudalism: Your lord lends you two cows. He takes most of the milk and leaves you some.

Pure Socialism: You have two cows. The government takes them and puts them into a barn with everyone else's cows. You have to take care of all the cows. The government gives you as much milk as you need.

Bureaucratic Socialism: You have two cows. The government takes them and puts them in a barn with everyone else's cows. They are cared for by ex-chicken farmers. You have to take care of the chickens the government took from the chicken farmers. The government gives you as much milk and eggs as the regulations say you need.

Fascism: You have two cows. The government takes them both, hires you to take care of them, and sells you the milk.

Pure Communism: You have two cows. Your neighbors help you to take care of them, and you all share the milk.

Russian Communism: You have two cows. You have to take care of them, but the government takes all the milk.

Cambodian Communism: You have two cows. The government takes them both and shoots you.

Dictatorship: You have two cows. The government takes them both and drafts you.

Pure Democracy: You have two cows. Your neighbors decide who gets the milk.

Representative Democracy: You have two cows. Your neighbors vote for someone to tell you who gets the milk.

American Democracy: The government promises to give you two cows if you vote for it. After the election, the President is impeached for speculating in cow futures. The press dubs the affair "Cowgate."

British Democracy: You have two cows. You feed them sheep brains and they go mad. The government doesn't do anything.

Bureaucracy: You have two cows. At first the government regulates what you can feed them and when you can milk them. Then it pays you not to milk them. Then it takes both, shoots one, milks the other and pours the milk down the drain. Then it requires you to fill out forms accounting for the missing cows.

Environmentalism: You have two cows. The government bans you from milking or killing them.

Pure Anarchy: You have two cows. Your neighbors riot and kill you for trying to sell the milk.

Libertarian/Anarcho-Capitalism: You have two cows. You sell one and buy a bull.

Clintonomics: You have two cows. The government requires you to take harmonica lessons.

Totalitarianism: You have two cows. The government takes them and denies they ever existed. Milk is banned.

Counter-Culture: Wow, dude, there's like... These two cows, man. You got to have some of this milk.

Hitler's belief in evolution rested in a philosophy which came from reading books like *Theozoology*.

"In Germany, they [the Gestapo] came first for the Communists, and I didn't speak up because I wasn't a Communist. Then they came for the Jews, and I didn't speak up because I wasn't a Jew. Then they came for the trade unionists, and I didn't speak up because I wasn't a trade unionist. Then they came for the Catholics, and I didn't speak up because I was a Protestant. Then they came for me, and by that time no one was left to speak up."
—Martin Niemoller, German Pastor before World War Two

"How fortunate for those in power that the people never think."
—Adolf Hitler

Hitler's Hit List

In Vienna from 1900 to 1918, a renegade Catholic monk, Adolf Lanz (nom de plume Lanz von Liebenfels), gave the Manichaean[1] cosmology a secular form. In preaching to his sect, The New Order of Templars, in his monthly journal Ostara and in his book Theozoology, Lanz taught that in the beginning there had been two earthly races: the Aryan[2] Heroes (Asings) and the Animal People (Apes). The Aryans were the earthly equivalent of the Manichaean light; they had been a divine race endowed with supremely intelligent, electronic minds, blond, blue-eyed beauty, and creativity.

The Animal People were the worldly counterparts of the Manichaean darkness; they had been a demonic race cursed with stupidity (except in the art of deception, in which they excelled), gorilla-like ugliness, and the urge to destroy. At some early time, the Apes began to envy and hate the Asings. They pondered methods of destroying the Aryans and decided to attack the superior race through miscegenation. Conveniently, the Aryan women had a fatal susceptibility to the Apes. (Lanz insisted that the story of the temptation of Eve in Genesis was an esoteric account of her seduction by one of the monsters.) After several centuries of such interbreeding, the original Asings and Animals disappeared. Now the earth was populated by mixed races, which could be ranked as higher or lower according to the proportions of Aryan and Ape blood that they possessed, approximately as follows:

Species	Blood Mixture
Nordic (blond, blue-eyed)	Close to pure Aryan
Germanic (brown hair, blue-eyed or, less desirable, brown-eyed)	Predominantly Aryan
Mediterranean (white but swarthy)	Slight Aryan preponderance
Slavic (white but degenerative bone structure)	Half Aryan, half Ape
Oriental	Slight Ape preponderance
Black African	Predominantly Ape
Jewish (fiendish skull)	Close to pure Ape

—from *The Hitler Movement*, p. 107

[1] **Manichaeanism:** a religious philosophy taught from the third to seventh centuries A.D. by the Persian Manes (or Manichaeus) and his followers, combining Zoroastrian, Gnostic Christian, and pagan elements, and based on the doctrine of the contending principles of good (light, God, the soul) and evil (darkness, Satan, the body).

[2] **Aryanism:** belief in the past existence of the hypothetical Aryan race supposedly possessing a superior civilization. (Aryan has no validity as a racial term, although so used notoriously by the Nazis to mean "a Caucasian of non-Jewish descent.")

NOTES

MISCELLANEOUS

"I think that the most important factor moving us toward a secular society has been the educational factor. Our schools may not teach Jonny how to read properly, but the fact that Jonny is in school until he is sixteen tends toward the elimination of religious superstition. The average American child now acquires a high school education, and this militates against Adam and Eve and all other myths of alleged history."

—P. Blanchard, "Three Cheers for Our Secular State," *The Humanist,* Jan/Feb 1983

4 Types of Workers

#1 **Sees a job and does it.** This kind of worker always becomes a boss or business owner and makes big bucks. The best workers do a job swiftly, cheerfully, humbly, and thoroughly. They are usually very happy and fulfilled in life. "Even a child is known by his doings, whether his work be pure, and whether it be right." "Prepare thy work without, and make it fit for thyself in the field; and afterwards build thine house." Prov. 20:11; 24:27

#2 **Asks what job to do next.** This kind of worker is rare, but is never out of work. The boss loves to have some of these people working for him.

#3 **Must be asked to do a job.** This kind of worker is the most common. He never excels in the job market and usually gripes about being overlooked when promotions are made. Some of these employees will work cheerfully (Type A) and some not cheerfully (Type B).

#4 **Must be found and asked to do a job.** This kind of worker gets minimum wage and never holds a job long. He is unhappy in life but cannot figure out why. "How long wilt thou sleep, O sluggard? when wilt thou arise out of thy sleep?" "The soul of the sluggard desireth, and hath nothing: but the soul of the diligent shall be made fat." Prov. 6:9; 13:4

Observations: If you are always being told what to do, you are not a #1 or #2 worker! The #3 and #4 workers often worsen with age. Each group can be further divided into subcategories, based on the person's ability and knowledge of the job. Some are eager to work but do not know what to do. God wants all of His children, to the best of their ability, to develop the talents He has given them.

See Dr. Hovind's video tape *How to Make Money and Spend It God's Way.* **Call or write for a free catalog.**

Comparing Honeybee Brain and Super Computer

"And in man is a three-pound brain which, as far as we know, is the most complex and orderly arrangement of matter in the universe."

—**Dr. Isaac Asimov**, in Smithsonian Institute Journal, June, 1970, p. 10-11. Former Professor, Boston School of Medicine, former atheist and humanist—now he knows better!

A Honeybee's Brain Compared to a Super Computer

Size	Tiny	Huge
Speed	1 trillion/sec	6 billion/sec*
Energy Consumption	10 Microwatts	many Kilowatts (10,000,000 or more)
Cost	Cheap	Lots ($48 million)
Maintanence Personnel	None (self healing)	Many
Weight	Not much	2,300 lbs
Conclusions:	Evolved?	Designed

The Human brain is millions of times more complex than a honeybee's.

*NASA's Y-MPC90

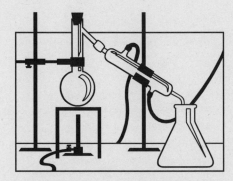

Carbon 14 Calibration Curve: How Carbon Dating Is Supposed to Work

A freshly killed seal was carbon dated as having died 1300 years ago!
—Antarctic Journal Vol. 6
Sept-Oct. 1971 p. 211

"A geologist at the Berkeley Geochronology Center, [Carl] Swisher uses the most advanced techniques to date human fossils. Last spring he was re-evaluating *Homo erectus* skulls found in Java in the 1930s by testing the sediment he found with them. A hominid species assumed to be an ancestor of *Homosapiens* "Erectus" was thought to have vanished some 250,000 years ago. But even though he used two different dating methods, Swisher kept making the same startling find: the bones were 53,000 years old at most and possibly no more than 27,000 years, a stretch of time contemporaneous with modern humans."
—Kaufman, Leslie, "Did a Third Human Species Live Among Us?" *Newsweek* (December 23, 1996), **p. 52.**

Radiocarbon dating was invented by Willard Libby in the early 1950s at the University of Chicago. While not totally useless, dating methods are overrated. Willard Libby said that carbon dating was only accurate for objects a few thousand years old.

Cosmic radiation strikes our atmosphere, changing the element Nitrogen (N_{14}) to Carbon 14 (C_{14}). This C_{14} is radioactive (can be detected by a Geiger counter). This radioactive carbon is mixed in with the normal carbon in the atmosphere, generally in the form of carbon dioxide (CO_2).

Plants intake carbon dioxide and make it part of their tissue. Animals eat the plants and the CO_2 becomes part of their body tissue. When the plant or animal dies it stops taking in new CO_2.

Radioactive carbon is very rare in the environment today (only .0000765%) and becomes even more rare as it decays into simpler components. About half of the C_{14} will break down (decay) into simpler components in about 5,730 years. This is called the half-life of C_{14}. In two "half-lives" (11,460 years), only one fourth of the original C_{14} will still be in an object. By using the number of clicks on the Geiger counter as a guide, scientists should be able to determine the age of an object. Because the atmosphere today will produce about 16 clicks per minute for each gram of carbon, the Geiger counter should click 8 times per minute if a sample is 5,730 years old and 4 clicks per minute if it is 11,460 years old.

While Carbon 14 dating sounds good so far, several faulty assumptions, which are listed on the following page, underlie the procedure. Most of the other radiometric dating methods use the same faulty assumptions. See Frequently Asked Question #3 (yellow pages) for examples of dates given by radiocarbon dating.

Tree Rings

Bible Parchment
Ptolemy
Redwood
Sesostris
Zoser
Hemaka

Absolute Specific Radioactivity

Years Before Present
45,000 40,000 35,000 30,000 25,000 20,000 15,000 10,000 5,000

Wrong Assumptions in C$_{14}$ Dating Methods

Living penguins have been carbon dated as being 8000 years old! (See frequently asked questions for more wild dates obtained by carbon dating.)

At least six different radiometric dating methods are available. *The assumed age of the sample will dictate which dating method is used because each will give a different result.*

For example: when dinosaur bones containing carbon are found, they are *not* carbon dated because the result would be only a few thousand years. Because this would not match the assumed age based on the geologic column, scientists use another method of dating to give an age closer to the desired result. All radiometric results that do not match the preassigned ages of the geologic column are discarded.

1. Atmospheric C$_{14}$ is in equilibrium. This assumption is wrong. It has been estimated that the C$_{14}$ in the earth's atmosphere would reach equilibrium (the formation rate would be equal to the decay rate) in about 30,000 years. The amount of C$_{14}$ in the atmosphere is still increasing. This research indicates a young earth (probably less than 10,000 years).

The same research also modifies all dates obtained by C$_{14}$ decay. As the earth's magnetic field decays, more cosmic radiation penetrates our atmosphere. On a Geiger counter, 16 clicks per minute per gram (16DPM/Gc) is typical in living objects today. Plants and animals that lived on the earth four thousand years ago would have had much less C$_{14}$ in their body to start with. The low amount of C$_{14}$ would make them appear to be thousands of years older than they really are. Several factors can affect the rate of C$_{14}$ formation. The 11-year solar sunspot cycle is one such factor.

2. Decay rate remains constant. Many times this assumption has been shown to be uncertain. Because the rate of decay may not be constant, dates obtained by C$_{14}$ may be accepted, but only with caution.

3. Initial amounts of C$_{14}$ can be known. Many times this assumption has been demonstrated to be wrong. Different parts of the same sample often yield different ratios. Various living samples give very different ratios. Some items will not be tested with carbon dating even though they contain carbon (see number 5 below). Would a mollusk have the same amount of C$_{14}$ per gram of carbon as a tree? Probably not. Living penguins have been carbon dated at 8000 years old! The oldest sample of independently known age is Hemaka, the Egyptian mummy from 2700–3100 B.C. (Secular writers of antiquity tend to exaggerate ages, so even these dates are suspect.)

4. The sample being tested has not been contaminated for thousands of years. This assumption is very difficult (if not impossible) to prove. Parent or daughter products may have leached in or out of the sample. Many lab tests have confirmed that this can happen.

5. The geologic column can be used as a base to calibrate the C$_{14}$ dates This assumption is not wise. The ages applied to the geologic column (invented in the 1800s to discredit the Bible) do not exist anywhere in the world except in textbooks. Poly-strata fossils, missing layers, layers out of order, misplaced fossils, and layers in reverse order all invalidate the geologic column (the Creation Seminar Tapes 4–6 have more information on this subject).

"Fundamentalist parents have no right to indoctrinate their children in their beliefs. We are preparing their children for the year 2,000 and life in a global one-world society and those children will not fit in."
—**Senator Paul Hoagland**, Nebraska, said to Everette Siliven's attorney, 1984

In 1959 President Eisenhower asked congress for $1 billion for the Department of Health Education & Welfare new American Education Fund for the promotion and publication of the new science of Evolution. $10,500,000 was given to the National Science Foundation (NSF) for the new 9 part theme curriculum, teaching evolution. The NSF provided the Biological Sciences Curriculum Study (BSCS) with the funds to provide the textbooks to public schools. The Changing Classroom: The Role Of The Biological Sciences Curriculum Study, Arnold B. Grobman, Doubleday & Co., NY 1969, pp 204, 26, 170, 200, 172; Scientists In The Classroom, pp 107, 109; Cornerstone Ministry 800-633-4369, lanekit@aol.com, Mr. Norris Anderson; CSS FreySci@aol.com.
Wisconsin Administrative Code 361 Rule The criteria for selection of textbooks...shall be: Factual accuracy.

This chart shows the number of words devoted to evolution in science textbooks during the last 40 years. The decline in the number of words after 1963 was because there was less content in general. The percentage of text devoted to evolution remained about the same.

Indoctrination in Evolution:
Before and After Federal Funding

Those who believe in the theory of evolution often complain that public school science textbooks do not present enough information on their theory. They say that students' science test scores are falling because of this lack of teaching evolution.

I believe that the opposite is true. Evolution has nothing to do with science and is anti-science. Students should spend time learning real science, not religious worldviews like evolution.

Evolutionary theory appears in nearly all subjects and grades in one form or another. Why? I believe one major reason is fear: When the Soviet Union launched Sputnik in 1957, some Americans panicked at the thought of losing the space race. A few dedicated humanists decided that America was behind because it was not teaching evolution as much as the Soviets were. The federal government began involvement in producing public school textbooks in the late 1950s (a clear violation of the Tenth Amendment to the U.S. Constitution).

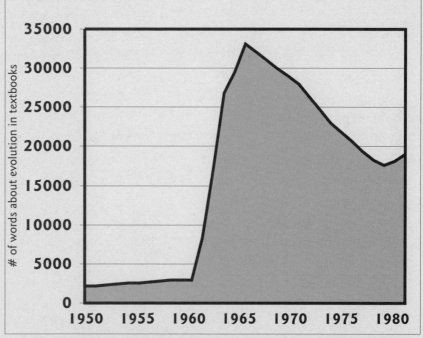

The charts on the following pages, showing the moral decline in America, reveal another side to the story. Contact Mel Gabler at 903- 753-5993 for more information on what is happening to textbooks in America. Call Dr. Kent Hovind for more information on Creation, evolution, and dinosaurs. Be sure to see the entire seminar series on videotape.

Sources:
c. 1948 Rand, Dynamic Biology Today
c. 1959 Harcourt, Exploring Biology, 5th
c. 1960 Holt, Modern Biology
c. 1961 Trial Ver. BSCS Green
c. 1961 Trial Ver. BSCS Blue
c. 1973 Houghton, BSCS Blue
c. 1980 Harcourt, BSCS Yellow
c. 1978 Rand, Dynamic Biology Today
c. 1980 Heath, BSCS Blue

Sexually Transmitted Diseases Gonorrhea:
Ages 15–16, Up 226%

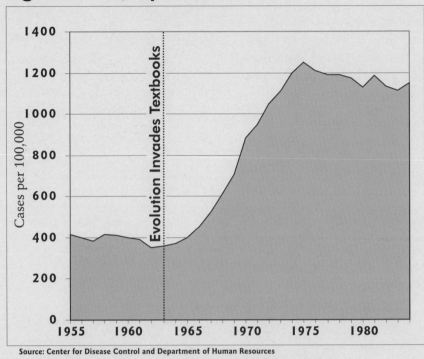

Cases per 100,000

Evolution Invades Textbooks

1400
1200
1000
800
600
400
200
0

1955   1960   1965   1970   1975   1980

Source: Center for Disease Control and Department of Human Resources

"Give me your four year olds, and in a generation I will build a socialist state."
—Vladimir Lenin

"The world has cancer, and the cancer is man."
—A. Gregg, *Mankind at the Turning Point*

Wallbuilders, Inc. P.O. Box 397, Aledo, TX 76008 Phone (817) 441-6044

Thanks for permission to use these charts.

Scholastic Aptitude Test
Scores: Decline in Student Achievement

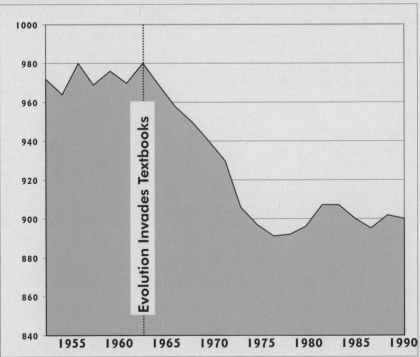

Evolution Invades Textbooks

1000
980
960
940
920
900
880
860
840

1955   1960   1965   1970   1975   1980   1985   1990

Source: College Entrance Exam Board

Violent Crime Offenses

"All the miseries and evils which men suffer from vice, crime, ambition, injustice, oppression, slavery, and war proceed from their despising or neglecting the precepts contained in the Bible."
—**Noah Webster,** Founding father and educator

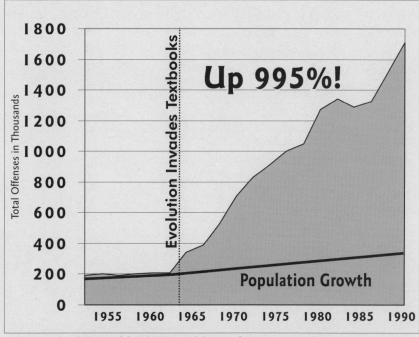

Total Offenses in Thousands

Up 995%!

Evolution Invades Textbooks

Population Growth

1955 1960 1965 1970 1975 1980 1985 1990

Source: *Statistical Abstracts of the United States*, and the Dept. of Commerce, Census Bureau

Unwed Birth Rates up 325%
Pregnancies to Girls 10–14 Up 553%*

"We have no government armed with power capable of contending with human passions unbridled by morality and religion. Avarice, ambition, revenge or gallantry would break the strongest cords of our Constitution as a whale goes through a net. Our Constitution was made only for a moral and religious people. It is wholly inadequate to the government of any other."
—**John Adams**

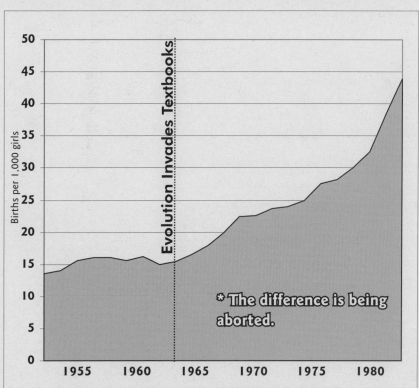

Births per 1,000 girls

Evolution Invades Textbooks

* The difference is being aborted.

1955 1960 1965 1970 1975 1980

Source: Dept. of Health and Human Resources and *Statistical Abstracts of the United States*

Divorce Rates

"[Jesus] saith unto them, Moses because of the hardness of your hearts suffered you to put away your wives: but from the beginning it was not so. And I say unto you, Whosoever shall put away his wife, except it be for fornication, and shall marry another, committeth adultery: and whoso marrieth her which is put away doth commit adultery."
—**Matthew 19:8-9**

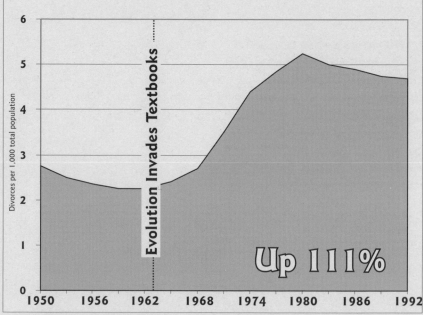

Source: US National Center for Health Statistics, Vital Statistics of the United States

"Destroy the family and society will collapse"
—**Vladimir Lenin**

Unmarried Couples

"In our country the lie has become not just a moral category, but a pillar of the state."
—**Alexander Solzhenitsyn**

Prior to 1977, unmarried couples living together was such a small group that data on this group was collected only in the ten year census reports.

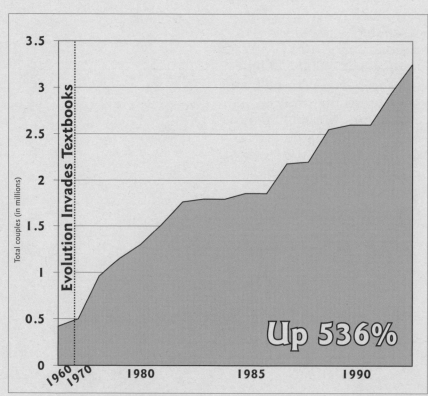

Source: Statistical Abstracts of the United States

Child Abuse

"And let us with caution indulge the supposition that morality may be maintained without religion. Whatever may be conceded to the influence of refined education on minds... reason and experience both forbid us to expect that national morality can prevail in exclusion of religious principle."
—**George Washington,** from "Farewell Address"

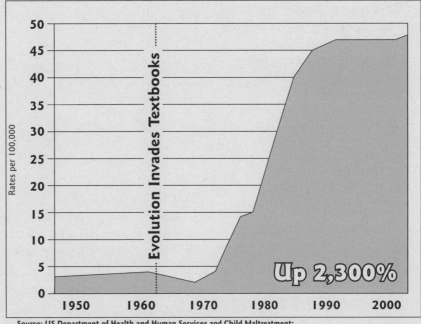

Source: US Department of Health and Human Services and Child Maltreatment: Reports from the States to the National Child Abuse and Neglect Data System.

Illegal Drug Usage
% youth who have used illegal drugs

"What constitutes the standard of good morals? Is it not Christianity? There certainly is none other. Say that cannot be appealed to, and I don't know what would be good morals. The day of moral virtue in which we live would, in an instant, if that standard were abolished, lapse into the dark and murky night of Pagan immorality."
— **Supreme Court of South Carolina**, 1846

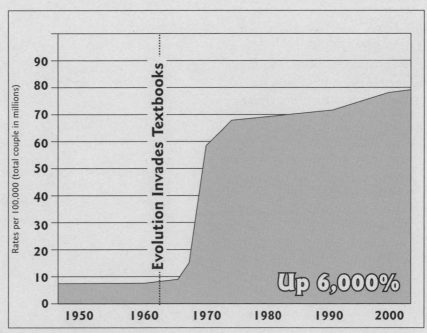

Source: National Institute on Drug Abuse

Human Population Chart

Is Earth really overcrowded? What is the motive for all of the overpopulation propaganda?

1. Devaluing human life
2. Justifying abortion
3. Scaring people into more government regulation
4. Causing acceptance of the Communist idea of taking from the rich to give to the poor

Earth has over 197,000,000 square miles of surface area, of which approximately 57,200,000 square miles, or 36,608,000,000 acres, is above water. With 6 billion people on the earth, every person could have nearly seven acres to himself. The entire world population could fit in a circle with an eleven mile radius. Everyone could fit twice within the city limits of Jacksonville, Florida (25 billion square feet).

Though much land surface is not inhabitable, Earth is not overcrowded. (Some areas are overcrowded.) Millions of people make their living from, and even live on, the water.

Earth, as originally created mostly land and small seas, could have supported a population of hundreds of billions, so it is clear God is not against large families (Gen. 1:26–28, 9:7, and Ps. 127:3–5). Truly, "He formed it [earth] to be inhabited..." (Is. 45:18).

> "Christianity is our foe. If animal rights is to succeed, we must destroy the Judeo-Christian Religious tradition."
> —**Peter Singer,** "Father of Animal Rights"

> "To compel a man to furnish contributions of money for the propagation of opinions which he disbelieves and abhors is sinful and tyrannical."
> —**Thomas Jefferson**

Scale: 2/3 inch = 1000 years

At this scale, the evolutionists' supposed origin of man, 3 million years ago, would be 125 feet to the left, and the imaginary Big Bang and forming of the Earth 4.6 billion years ago would be 36 miles to the left of this chart.

Estimated Population ¼ billion

Noah's Flood (8 Survivors)

2000	6
1985	5
1977	4
1962	3
1930	2
1800	1

4000 BC   3000 BC   2000 BC   1000 BC   Birth of Christ   1000 AD   2000 AD

How much is a billion?

Adam was created 189 **billion** seconds ago—
3.2 billion minutes ago
52.6 million hours ago
2.2 million days ago

Jesus was born 62.8 **billion** seconds ago—
1 billion minutes ago
17.5 million hours ago
.73 million days ago

FREQUENTLY ASKED QUESTIONS

"Wherefore God also gave them up to uncleanness through the lusts of their own hearts, to dishonour their own bodies between themselves: Who changed the truth of God into a lie, and worshipped and served the creature more than the Creator, who is blessed for ever. Amen."

—Romans 1:24-25

Question List

It has been my custom since I began the ministry of Creation Science Evangelism in 1989, to have an open time for questions and answers during my seminars. I tell the audience that any question is fair game. Over the years, many interesting questions have been asked. Here are some of the questions that have come my way in seminars or by mail and my answers. I'm sure we will be adding to this section until the Lord comes back. Please feel free to send in your question if you don't see it here or call in today to our world-wide radio program. (See our web site www.drdino.com for contact information.)

Many of these questions and scores of others, are dealt with in more detail with visuals on my video tape #7 of the creation seminar series. Other questions about subjects such as the dinosaurs, cave men, fire breathing dragons, why the pre-flood people lived over 900 years, what caused the flood, the ice age and many others are dealt with in the first 6 tapes of the series. The questions below are in categories and numbered for easier reference.

I. General science questions:

1. Why do creationists fight against science?
2. How do we see stars billions of light years away?
3. Doesn't carbon dating prove the Earth is old?
4. The number of fossils in certain areas of the world is enormous. How could the earth have supported all those creatures at the same time?
5. Is man evolving bigger and smarter?
6. Was the earth ever a hot, molten mass like the textbooks say?
7. How are diamonds, oil, fossil fuels and natural gas formed?
8. How do you explain the formation of fine strata layers called varves, such as those in the Green River formation in Wyoming, which contains 20 million fine layers which represent 1 year each? Doesn't this prove the earth is more than 6,000 years old?
9. What about black holes?
10. What about the Mars rock? Is there or was there life on Mars?

II. Public schools questions:

11. Should (or can) creation science be taught in the public school system?
12. What can public school kids and their parents do about evolution being taught in the public school system?

> "Evolution is unproved and unprovable. We believe it only because the only alternative is special creation, and that is unthinkable."
> —**Sir Arthur Keith** in the forward to the 100th anniversary edition of Darwin's book, *Origin of Species* in 1959

> "Evolution is a fairy tale for grownups. The theory has helped nothing in the progress of science. It is useless."
> —**Professor Louis Bounoure** Director of the Strasbourg Zoological Museum

> "I myself am convinced that the theory of evolution, especially the extent to which it has been applied, will be one of the great jokes in the history books of the future. Posterity will marvel that so flimsy and dubious an hypothesis could be accepted with the incredible credulity that it has."
> —**Malcolm Muggeridge** journalist and philosopher, Pascal Lectures, University of Waterloo, Ontario, Canada

"The assumption of continuity (a continuous distribution of animal forms reflected in the fossil record) is crucial to Darwinian theory. The fossil record does not appear to support the assumption of evolutionary theory, or anything much like it."
—David Berlinski, September, 1996

"Lynn Margolis is a Distinguished University Professor of Biology at the University of Massachusetts... At one of her many public talks she asks the molecular biologists in the audience to name a single, unambiguous example of the formation of a new species by the accumulation of mutations. Her challenge goes unmet."
—M. J. Behe, *Darwin's Black Box,* 1996 p.26

P. 56. "Even the nearest Capheids are so remote that it is difficult to determine their absolute distances with any great accuracy.... "All large distances ... in astronomical literature ... subject to an error of perhaps 10 per cent, from this cause alone." p. 61. "We now know that faintness arises from two causes [distance and absorbing matter in space], and it is not generally possible to apportion it accurately between the two." Jeans, James,
—The Universe Around Us (New York: Cambridge University Press, 1969)

III. Bible questions:

13. Are there contradictions in the Bible?
14. Where did the races come from?
15. Is there any scientific explanation for the opening of the Red Sea and Moses leading the children of Israel across the bottom?
16. Is God getting old?
17. When were angels created?
18. What is the unicorn mentioned in the Bible?
19. When did Satan fall?
20. How old was Terah when Abram was born?

IV. Flood questions:

21. Did it rain before the flood?
22. How did Noah take care of all those animals on the ark?
23. Did Noah take millions of insects on the ark?
24. How did animals travel from all over to get to the ark?
25. What about dinosaurs? Did they live with Adam and Eve? Did Noah take them on the ark?
26. It would take 4.4 billion cubic kilometers of water to cover Mt. Everest. Where did the water come from to flood the earth?
27. During the flood, how did the fresh water fish survive?
28. If there was really a world-wide flood where are all the bones of the humans that drowned?

V. Miscellaneous Questions:

29. What is the Gaia Hypothesis?
30. What about the ozone hole, and R-12 refrigerants?
31. What about global warming?
32. Who built the Great Pyramid, and why?
33. What is the Bermuda triangle?
34. What about Big-foot?
35. What about UFO's?
36. Is it possible for your television to watch you?
37. What about the Mark of the Beast?
38. How would you answer critics like Matson, Babinski and Bartelt who have written bad things about you?
39. How are evolution, Communism, the new-world order and the IRS connected?
40. Where did you get your degree?

NOT to scale

General science questions:

1. Q: Why do creationists fight against science?

A: Your question has me confused. All major branches of science were started by creationists. There has never been one advancement in any field of science that the evolution theory has helped. The evolution theory is useless. I don't know of any creations who fights against science. I certainly love science and taught it for 15 years. Most creationists that I know love science and only fight against evolution. You may be confusing the evolution theory with science. Some think the two go together. This is a common mistake due to the intense evolution propaganda campaign of the last 50 years. It would help if you watch my videotape #4 for more on this. There has never been any evidence that any kind of plant or animal has ever been able to create itself or produce any other kind of plant or animal. We have seen thousands of changes within the created kinds but that is not evolution. Please don't accuse me of being against science. I am only against the false teaching of evolution as science.

2. Q: If the earth is only 6000 years old, how is it we can see stars that are billions of light years away?

A: This is one of the most commonly asked questions and deserves an honest answer. Below is first a short answer then a more thorough answer. There are three things we need to consider when answering the starlight question.

1.Scientists cannot measure distances beyond 100 light years accurately.

2. No one knows what light is or that it always travels the same speed throughout all time, space and matter.

3. The creation was finished or mature when God made it. Adam was full-grown, the trees had fruit on them, the starlight was visible, etc.

Let me elaborate on these 3 points. First, no one can measure star distance accurately. The farthest accurate distance man can measure is 20 light years (some textbooks say up to 100), not several billion light years. Man measures star distances using parallax trigonometry. By choosing two measurable observation points and making an imaginary triangle to a third point, and using simple trigonometry, man calculates the distance to the third point. The most distant observation points available to an earth bound observer are the positions of the earth in solar orbit six months apart, say June and December. This would create a

Previous page's drawing to scale
(16 light minutes across, 525,948 minutes long)

Sun

Earth
in
December

Earth
in
June

triangle of 186,000,000 miles, which equals only 16 light minutes. There are 525,948 minutes in a year. Even if the nearest star were only one light year away (and it is much further), the angle at the third point measures .017 degrees. In simpler terms, a triangle like this would be the same angle two surveyors would see if they were standing sixteen inches apart and focusing on a third point 525,948 inches or 8.30 miles away. If they stayed 16 inches apart and focused on a dot 830 miles away, they would have the same angle as an astronomer measuring a point 100 light years away. A point 5 million light years away is impossible to figure with trigonometry. The stars may be that far away but modern man has no way of measuring those great distances. No one can state definitively the distance to the stars.

Several other methods such as luminosity and red shift are employed to try to guess at greater distances but all such methods have serious problems and assumptions involved. For a more complex and slightly different answer to the star light question from another Christian perspective, see the book Starlight and Time by Russel Humphry available from www.icr.org.

Second, the speed of light may not be a constant. It does vary in different media (hence the rainbow effect of light going through a prism) and may also vary in different places in space. The entire idea behind the black hole theory is that light can be attracted by gravity and be unable to escape the great pull of these imaginary black holes. No one knows what light is let alone that it's velocity has been the standard of time, if the speed of light is decaying, the clock would be changing at the same rate and therefore not be noticed as the following demonstrate: June 4, 2000, the following article appeared in the Sunday Times from UK. "Eureka! Scientists Break Speed of Light" Jonathan Leake, Science Editor June 4, 2000 United States.

SCIENTISTS claim they have broken the ultimate speed barrier: the speed of light. In research carried out in the United States, particle physcists have shown that light pulses can be accelarated to up to 300 times their normal velocity of 186,000 miles per second.

The work was carried out by Dr. Lijun Wang, of the NEC research institute in Princeton, who transmitted a pulse of light towards a chamber filled with specially treated cesium gas. Se also; New York Times May 30, 2000. Www.nytimes.com

See Seminar 7 and FAQ on our website for much more.

3. Q: Doesn't carbon dating prove the earth is millions of years old?

A: Whenever the worldview of evolution is questioned, this topic always comes up. Let's look at how carbon dating works and the assumptions it is based on.

"Facts do not cease to exist because they are ignored."
—**Aldous Huxley**

"The collective needs of non-human species must take precedence over the needs and desires of humans."
—**Dr. Reed F. Noss,** The Wildlands Project

"A team led by Nail R. Tanvir of the University of Cambridge in England used a two step method to estimate the [Hubble] constant. First they observed a type of "standard candle"-stars known as Cepheid variables-to find the distance to the spiral galaxy M96... You have to be very careful about [drawing conclusions] because all of the [Hubble constant] measurements have huge systematic errors."
—**Science News** Sept. 9, 1995 p. 166

"Radiocarbon is forming 28-37% faster than it is decaying"
—**R.E. Taylor** et al., American Antiquity, Vol. 50, No. 1 1985 pp. 136-140

"Living mollusk shells were dated up to 2300 years old."
—**Science vol.** 141, 1963 p. 634-637

"Basalt from Mt. Etna, Sicily (122 BC) gave K-AR age of 250,000 years old. Dalyrmple, G.B., 1969 40Ar/36Ar analysis of historic lava flows."
—**Earth and Planetary Science Letters,** 6-47 55. See also: Impact #307 Jan. 1999

Radiation from the sun strikes the atmosphere of the earth all day long. This energy converts about 21 pounds of nitrogen into radioactive carbon 14. This radioactive carbon 14 slowly decays back into normal, stable nitrogen. Extensive laboratory testing has shown that about half of the C-14 molecules will decay in 5730 years. This is called the half-life. After another 5730 years half of the remaining C-14 will decay leaving only ¼ of the original C-14. It goes from ½ to ¼ to 1/8, etc. In theory it would never totally disappear, but after about 5 half lives the difference is not measurable with any degree of accuracy. This is why most people say carbon dating is only good for objects less than 40,000 years old. Nothing on earth carbon dates in the millions of years, because the scope of carbon dating only extends a few thousand years. Willard Libby invented the carbon dating technique in the early 1950's. The amount of carbon 14 in the atmosphere today is about .0000765%. It is assumed there would be the same amount found in living plants or animals since the plants breath CO_2 and animals eat plants.

Since sunlight causes the formation of C-14 in the atmosphere, and normal radioactive decay takes it out, there must be a point where the formation rate and the decay rate equalizes. This is called the point of equilibrium. Let me illustrate: If you were trying to fill a barrel with water but there were holes drilled up the side of the barrel, as you filled the barrel it would begin leaking out the holes. At some point you would be putting it in and it would be leaking out at the same rate. You will not be able to fill the barrel past this point of equilibrium. In the same way the C-14 is being formed and decaying simultaneously. A freshly created earth would require about 30,000 years for the amount of C-14 in the atmosphere to reach this point of equilibrium because it would leak out as it is being filled. Tests indicate that the earth has still not reached equilibrium. There is more C-14 in the atmosphere now than there was 40 years ago. This would prove the earth is not yet 30,000 years old! This also means that plants and animals that lived in the past had less C-14 in them than do plants and animals today. Just this one fact totally upsets data obtained by C-14 dating.

The carbon in the atmosphere normally combines with oxygen to make carbon dioxide (CO_2). Plants breathe CO_2 and make it part of their tissue. Animals eat the plants and make it part of their tissues. A very small percentage of the carbon plants take in is radioactive C-14. When a plant or animal dies it stops taking in air and food so it should not be able to get any new C-14. The C-14 in the plant or animal will begin to decay back to normal nitrogen. The older an object is, the less carbon-14 it contains. One gram of carbon from living plant material causes a Geiger counter to click 16 times per minute as the C-14 decays. A sample that causes 8 clicks per minute would be 5,730 years old (the sample has gone through one half life). and so on. (See chart on page 45 about C-14).

"In the last two years an absolute date has been obtained for (the Ngandong beds, above the Trinil beds), and it has the very interesting value of 300,000 years plus or minus 300,000 years."
—**Birdsell, J. B.,** *Human Evolution* (Chicago: Rand McNally, 1975), p. 295

"One part of Dima [a baby frozen mammoth] was 40,000, another part was 26,000 and the 'wood immediately around the carcass' was 9-10,000."
—**Troy L. Pewe,** *Quaternary Stratigraphic Nomenclature in Unglaciated Central Alaska,* Geological Survey Professional Paper 862 (U.S. Gov. printing office, 1975) p. 30

"The lower leg of the Fairbanks Creek mammoth had a radiocarbon age of 15,380 RCY, while its skin and flesh were 21,300 RCY."
—**Harold E. Anthony,** "Natures Deep Freeze," *Natural History,* Sept. 1949, p. 300 See also: *In the Beginning* Walt Brown p. 124

Although this technique looks good at first, carbon-14 dating rests on at least two simple assumptions. They are, obviously, assuming the amount of carbon-14 in the atmosphere has always been constant, and its rate of decay has always been constant. Neither of these assumptions is provable or reasonable. An illustration may help: Imagine you found a candle burning in a room, and you wanted to determine how long it was burning before you found it. You could measure the present height of the candle (say, seven inches) and the rate of burn (say, an inch per hour). In order to find the length of time since the candle was lit we would be forced to make some assumptions. We would, obviously, have to assume that the candle has always burned at the same rate, and assume an initial height of the candle. The answer changes based on the assumptions. Similarly, scientists do not know that the carbon-14 decay rate has been constant. They do not know that the amount of carbon-14 in the atmosphere is constant. Present testing shows the amount of C-14 in the atmosphere has been increasing since it was first measured in the 1950's. This may be tied in to the declining strength of the magnetic field.

In addition to the above assumptions, dating methods are all subject to the geologic column date to verify their accuracy. If a date obtained by radiometric dating does not match the assumed age from the geologic column the radiometric date will be rejected. The so-called geologic column was developed in the early 1800's over a century before there were any radiometric dating methods. "Apart from very 'modern' examples, which are really archaeology, I can think of no cases of radioactive decay being used to date fossils."Ager, Derek V., "Fossil Frustrations," New Scientist, vol. 100 (November 10, 1983), p. 425. Laboratories will not carbon date dinosaur bones (even frozen ones which could easily be carbon dated) because dinosaurs are supposed to have lived 70 million years ago according to the fictitious geologic column. An object's supposed place on the geologic column determines the method used to date it. There are about 7 or 8 radioactive elements that are used today to try to date objects. Each one has a different half-life and a different range of ages it is supposed to be used for. No dating method cited by evolutionists is unbiased. For more information, see video tape #7 of the CSE video series on Creation, Evolution, and Dinosaurs; Bones of Contention by Marvin Lubenow, or Scientific Creationism by Henry Morris (all available from CSE).

A few examples of wild dates by radiometric dating:

Shells from living snails were carbon dated as being 27,000 years old. Science vol. 224, 1984, pp. 58-61

Living mollusk shells were dated up to 2300 years old. Science vol. 141, 1963, pp.634-637

"The two Colorado Creek mammoths had radiocarbon ages of 22,850 ±670 and 16,150 ± 230 years respectively."
—**Robert M. Thorson and R. Dale Guthrie**, "Stratigraphy of the Colorado Creek Mammoth Locality, Alaska," *Quaternary Research, Vol. 37, No. 2, March 1992, pp. 214-228,* see also: *In the Beginning* Walt Brown p. 244-246

"A geologist at the Berkeley Geochronology Center, [Carl] Swisher uses the most advanced techniques to date human fossils. Last spring he was re-evaluating *Homo erectus* skulls found in Java in the 1930s by testing the sediment found with them. A hominid species assumed to be an ancestor of *Homo sapiens,* "erectus was thought to have vanished some 250,000 years ago. But even though he used two different dating methods, Swisher kept making the same startling find: the bones were 53,000 years old at most and possibly no more than 27,000 years— a stretch of time contemporaneous with modern humans."
—**Leslie Kaufman,** "Did a Third Human Species Live Among Us?" *Newsweek* (December 23, 1996), p. 52.

A freshly killed seal was carbon dated as having died 1300 years ago! Antarctic Journal vol. 6, Sept-Oct. 1971, p.211

"One part of the Vollosovitch mammoth carbon dated at 29,500 years and another part at 44,000." Troy L. Pewe, "Quaternary Strigraphic Nomencature in Uniglaciated Central Alaska," Geologic Survey Professional Paper 862 (U.S. Gov. Printing Office, 1975) p. 30

"Structure, metamorphism, sedimentary reworking, and other complications have to be considered. Radiometric dating would not have been feasible if the geologic column had not been erected first." J. E. O'Rourke, "Pragmatism vs. Materialism in Stratigraphy," American Journal of Science, vol. 276 (January,1976), p. 54

Material from layers where dinosaurs are found carbon dated at 34,000 years old. Earth's Most Challenging Mysteries, 1972, p.280

4. Q: The number of fossils in certain areas of the world is enormous. How could earth have supported all those creatures at the same time?

A: This question shows a common false assumption that many people make. They assume the earth today is the same as it has always been. Today's earth is 70% under water. There are scriptural and scientific indications that the pre-flood world had greater air pressure, higher percentages of oxygen and carbon dioxide, much more land (above sea level), less water (on the earth's surface), and a canopy of water to filter out the harmful effects of the sun. This would cause there to be many times more plants and animals on the earth than there are today. The added air pressure would diffuse more gasses into the water and support a much greater fish population. Aquatic plant life per cubic mile would multiply also. II Peter 3 tells us that the scoffers in the last days will be willingly ignorant of how God created the heavens and the earth. They would also be ignorant of the flood. These two great events must be considered before making any statements about the conditions on earth today. Only about 3% of the earth today is habitable for man. The rest is under water, ice, deserts, mountains, etc. If the earth before the flood were for example, 70% habitable, it could have supported a huge population. Most of the water in today's oceans would been under the Earth's crust before the flood. See Psalm 24:1 and Psalm 136:7.

The vast amount and world-wide distribution of fossils shows the flood was global and that God hates sin enough to judge the entire world. See videos #2 and #6 of our Seminar Series for much more on this topic.

"If you will not fight for the right when you can easily win without bloodshed, if you will not fight when your victory will be sure and not so costly, you may come to the moment when you will have to fight with all the odds against you and only a precarious chance of survival. There may be a worse case. You may have to fight when there is no chance of victory, because it is better to perish than to live as slaves."
—Winston Churchill

"Those who hold tolerance as their highest virtue do so because they have no others."
—G. K. Chesterson

"Lava from the 1801 Hawaiian volcano eruption gave a K-Ar date of 1.6 Million years old.
Dalyrmple, G.B., 1969 40Ar/36Ar analysis of historic lava flows."
—*Earth and Planetary Science Letters*, 6-47 55. See also: *Impact #307* Jan. 1999

5. Q: Is man evolving bigger and smarter?

A: The evolution theory teaches that man has been improving over the last 3 million years. Nothing could be farther from the truth. Both history and scripture indicate that before the flood in the days of Noah people were much bigger and smarter than the average person is today. The Bible says they were living to be more than 900 years old. I show some of the evidence for giant humans on my video tape #2. As for smarter, you could learn a lot in 900 years! Plus, Adam came from the hand of God fully programmed with language capacity and the ability to classify or sort items quickly (he named all the animals in one day). Adam was around for over half of the time from the creation to the flood, so his great knowledge could be spread throughout the world.

In the last 400 years there has been a great increase in accumulated technology. This is not the same as wisdom or intelligence. We can have a computer because thousands of men before have invented various parts and ideas that can be put together. There is no evidence that modern man is smarter than ancient man. I think the opposite is true. Many of the ancient structures indicate greater intelligence in solving problems in a low-tech age. (See seminar 7 for more.)

As for man getting bigger, there has been an increase in average size over the last few hundred years in industrialized countries due to improved diet, sanitation, medicine, etc but this is not to be confused with evolution. Also the trend in bigger people is not proof of long-term growth patterns. If man today is say 8 inches taller than average man during the American Revolution 200 years ago it, obviously, would not prove that man was 80 inches shorter 2000 years ago or 800 inches shorter 20,000 years ago! Every age has seen both tall people and smart people. There is no evidence that modern man is any better.

6. Q: Was the earth ever a hot, molten mass like the textbooks say?

A: Evolutionists teach that the earth was a boiling hot, molten mass that slowly cooled down over millions of years. The Bible says in Genesis chapter 1 that "In the beginning God created the heaven and the earth…and the Spirit of God moved upon the face of the waters." So the surface of the earth was covered with water; it could not have been a hot, molten mass.

There is scientific evidence to support the Biblical account. Robert Gentry of Knoxville, Tennessee, does amazing research on radio-polonium halos in granite rock. Polonium is a rare element that is radioactive; it breaks down or decays like uranium. But polonium only lasts a few minutes. As it breaks down, it sends off little particles that fly a certain distance. An

"The people of these United States are the rightful masters of both Congress and the courts, not to overthrow the Constitution, but to overthrow the men who pervert the Constitution."
—Abraham Lincoln

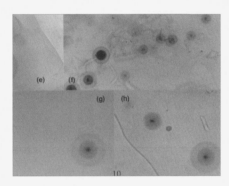

Radio polonium halos in granite rock prove the earth was never a molten mass.

"...the theory of evolution, a theory universally accepted not because it can be proven by logically coherent evidence to be true, but because the only alternative, special creation, is clearly incredible."
—Watson, 1929, p. 233

analogy would be a fireworks display that produces a sphere of fragments that only lasts a fraction of a second before it collapses. Different elements have fragments that fly different distances, each radioactive element has a particular "signature" (how big a circle it can make in the rock as it decays like a more powerful fireworks rocket would produce a bigger sphere in the air). Radio-active polonium, when it decays in a solid rock, makes a perfect sphere as it decays because all its fragments fly about the same distance from the center. If it decays in solid rock, the circle is preserved. But if it decays in a hot molten rock, the circle disappears. All over the world radio-polonium halos exist in granite, indicating the earth was never a hot, molten mass. See Robert Gentry's book Creation's Tiny Mystery, available from CSE - $13.50, for much more on this subject, or www.halos.com.

It is also interesting that Gentry's research was published in many major science magazines until someone realized that it was proving the big bang theory to be a big dud. The censorship of his valuable material by mainstream science magazines is incredible but predictable. Evolution is a very carefully protected state religion in this humanist world today.

7. Q: How are diamonds, oil, fossil fuels and natural gas formed?

A: Coal comes from massive amounts of trees and plant matter that has been changed by tremendous heat and pressure. Oil and natural gas form from fish, reptile, and animal matter under similar heat and pressure conditions. The most logical time for coal, oil and gas to form was during and after the world-wide flood, when enormous amounts of animal and vegetable matter underwent mass burial under the incredible destruction and pressure of the flood waters and the sediments. See www. answersingenesis.org for article "How fast can oil form."

Diamonds are highly pressurized, pure carbon gems. (Superman used to make them from coal all the time.) Most diamonds appear in "blue ground," in or near the neck of an extinct volcano where magma erupted. The high pressure of volcanic activity could have formed diamonds. Many may have formed when the "fountains of the deep" were broken up or when mountains arose during the last months of the flood" (Psalm 104:6-8.)

8. Q: How do you explain the formation of fine strata layers called varves such as those in the Green River formation in Wyoming which contains 20 million fine layers which represent 1 year each? Doesn't this prove the earth is more than 6,000 years old?

A: Like many questions posed by evolutionists, one has a built-in faulty assumption. This question assumes that each of these layers is annual, and this is, obviously, not the case.

In 1770 George Buffon said the earth was 70,000 years old.
—*Integrated Principals of Zoology* 1996 P. 151.
In 1905 the age of the earth was officially 2 billion years old. *Newsweek July 20, 1998 p. 50.* Today students are taught it is 4.6 billion years old. That means the earth has been getting older at the rate of 21 million years per year for the last 220 years! That's 40 years/min! We are aging fast!

"In the six hundredth year of Noah's life in the second month, the seventeenth day of the month, the same day were all the fountains of the great deep broken up, and the windows of heaven were opened"
—**Genesis 7:11**

"In the beginning of change, the patriot is a scarce man, and brave and hated and scorned. When his cause succeeds, the timid join him, for then it costs nothing to be a patriot."
—**Mark Twain**

Numerous experiments have been done on the formation. You can take a section of Green River formation and grind it to powder, drop it into moving water and it will resort itself into many fine layers. It has been shown that the layers are not annual at all. There are places in this formation where over 1500 layers are found in some areas and only 1000 in others, all between the same two ash layers called "event horizons." See Creation Magazine June-Aug. 1997. This subject is dealt with in great detail at the Institute for Creation Research (619) 448-0900, or visit their website at www.icr.org.

9. Q: What about black holes?

A: In order to escape the gravitational pull of the earth, a rocket must go 25,000 miles per hour. If it goes less than this it will fall back down. This speed is known as the escape velocity of earth. If a planet has stronger gravity, the escape velocity will be even greater.

The theory behind a black hole is the idea that if enough mass is in one location, the gravity would be so great that the escape velocity would be 186,000 miles per second so that even light could not escape. This, of course, is assuming that light can be effected by gravity. No one has ever seen a black hole since no light could escape one if it existed.

The problem black holes are supposed to fix is this: if the big bang theory were true, the matter should be evenly distributed in space. Since matter is not evenly distributed in space (we have clumps of matter called galaxies then zillions of miles of nothing between) the believers in the big bang theory are trying to explain why. They are trying to say: "There is matter in between the clumps but we can't see it because it is in black holes." Actually, they are arguing from a lack of evidence not from evidence. This is a poor position to be in when trying to prove your case in a court of law.

I don't know if black holes exist or not, but their existence is not proven.

10. Q: What about the Mars rock; is/was there life on Mars?

A: Life does not exist on Mars. The purpose of the Mars rock hype a few years ago was to help NASA get its grant money which has been stalled Congress. They must find something important with all the billions they spend. The rock had been found 7 years earlier near the South Pole. It arrived 13,000 years ago, according to NASA: In 13,000 years it could easily have become contaminated with Earth life. Or, in passing through the 200 mile thick Earth atmosphere, the rock could have become contaminated.

Also, the rock's supposed Mars origin is suspect. Suppose we reduce Earth to the size of a 4 inch tomato and Mars to the size of a 2 inch tomato; using this scale, the tomatoes would

"When it gets dark enough you can see the stars."
—**Ralph Waldo Emerson**

"Complex technology of any sort is an assault on human dignity. It would be little short of disastrous for us to discover the source of clean, cheap, abundant energy, because of what we might do with it."
—**Amory Lovins,** Rocky Mountain Institute

"Good intentions will always be pleaded for every assumption of power... It is hardly too strong to say that the Constitution was made to guard the people against the dangers of good intentions. There are men in all ages who mean to govern well, but they mean to govern. They promise to be good masters, but they mean to be masters."
—**Daniel Webster**

be 2,000 feet apart, over one-third of a mile at the closest point of their orbits. Suppose that you had to shoot the Mars tomato so that one piece of it landed on the Earth tomato, without leaving a dent in the Mars tomato. Highly unlikely, don't you think? Mars has no giant crater that would indicate it had been hit with enough force to knock a fragment all the way to earth. The whole purpose of the highly publicized Mars find was to push a NASA funding grant through Congress. It worked. The grant money was released, and, shortly thereafter, the announcement was made that the shape they had seen on the rock was "actually lamellae-fractured surfaces of pyroxene and carbonate crystals which were formed by geologic processes" according to a study led by John Bradley of the Georgia Institute of Technology. See Aviation Week and Space Technology, Dec. 8, 1997. For more on this topic see the book That Their Words May Be Used Against Them, by Dr. Henry Morris, available from CSE - $19.50.

Public School Questions:

11. Q: Should (or can) creation science be taught in the public school system?

A: This is a good question and it deserves a good answer, however, there are other questions that must be answered first before this question can be properly answered.

The first of these is: Should we have a public school system? The tenth amendment to the U.S. Constitution says, "The powers not delegated to the United States by the Constitution, nor prohibited by it to the States, are reserved to the States respectively, or to the people." The interference of the Federal government in the education of children in unconstitutional. I believe if the government was out of the education business (as well as welfare and hundreds of other socialist programs they have gotten into), many other problems would be eliminated and questions like this would be moot.

A second question to answer is: If we decide to have a public school system, who should run it? This will further eliminate questions about what is taught. If the local community wants to impart their values to the students, and they are paying the salaries, then their values should be taught. It is unfair and illegal (constitutionally) to force everyone (via taxes) to pay to have all children taught things contrary to the beliefs and values of their parents. The schools became public in the mid 1800's as part of a long-range plan for a new world order. See the article, "Why the Schools Went Public" by Samuel Blumenfeld (310) 391-2245 for more on this.

Now, to finally answer the question: Not only can you legally teach creation science in the public schools, you can teach it right out of the Bible, and teach or devote a class to religion, and have the textbook be the Bible. We all know the effects of what happened in 1963 when the Bible was taken out, and

"It has never been against the law to teach creation. No statute exists in any state to bar instruction in 'creation science.' It could be taught before, and it can be taught now."
—**Stephen Jay Gould** *"The Verdict on Creationism," New York Times* July 19, 1987, p. 34

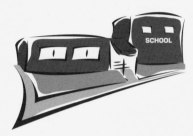

"The Supreme Court ruling did not, in any way, outlaw the teaching of 'creation science' in public school classrooms. Quite simply it ruled that, in the form taken by the Louisiana law, it is unconstitutional to demand equal time for this particular subject. 'Creation science' can still be brought into science classrooms If and when teachers and administrators feel that it is appropriate. Numerous surveys have shown that teachers and administrators favor just this route. And, in fact, 'creation science' is being taught in science courses throughout the country."
—**Evolutionary biologist Michael Zimmerman,** "Keep Guard Up After Evolution Victory," *BioScience* 37 (9, October 1987): 636

The Supreme Court stated that, "the Bible may constitutionally be used in an appropriate study of history, civilization, ethics, comparative religion, or the like."
—**Stone v. Graham,** 449 U.S. 39, 42 (1980)

evolution put in to the schools, but we have been deceived by that ACLU again! In 1963, the Supreme Court banned the use of the Bible to try to get kids saved, which is not good obviously, but it's a lot better than what the ACLU has led us to believe. They did not throw the Bible out! We have thrown the Bible out because we have allowed ourselves to be deceived by the ACLU.

In the landmark ruling of School District of Abington Township v. Schempp, 374 U.S. 203, 225, (1963) the court held that, "it certainly may be said that the Bible is worthy of study for its literary and historic qualities. Nothing we have said here indicates that such study of the Bible or of religion, when presented objectively as part of a secular program of education, may be effected consistently with the First Amendment."

In the ruling of Stone v. Graham, 449 U.S. 39, 42 (1980), The Supreme Court stated that, "the Bible may constitutionally be used in an appropriate study of history, civilization, ethics, comparative religion, or the like."

In Florey v. Sioux Falls School District, 619 F.2d 1311, 1314 (8th Cir, 1980), the court found that permitting public school observances which include religious elements promotes the secular purpose of "advancing the student's knowledge and appreciation of the role that our religious heritage has played in the social, cultural and historical development of civilization."

There are at least two other cases where the Supreme Court has ruled that the Bible may be used in its entirety for secular educational purposes such as: history, civilization, ethics, comparative religion, culture, and the morals on which this country was founded!

The Supreme Court never kicked the Bible out of schools in 1963. The problem is: We, Christians, who believed the lie that they did! The teachers are not allowed to try to convert students while on school time and property, but they can present creation. Now, I understand that not being able to use the Bible to get people saved is discouraging, but, being able to use it to teach creation science or the morals that this country was founded on can and will reverse the current indoctrination! You cannot only teach creation science, you can do it right from the Bible – verse by verse – or you could go out on a different subject and teach how the Bible is the only moral absolute that this country has. This country was founded on the morals in the Bible, and without the Bible, all morals are in-absolute, and are subject to some human's interpretation! You can teach that! If you get in trouble (and there is a risk because so many principals have been misled or intimidated by ACLU type lawyers) call ACLJ (American Center for Law and Justice in Virginia– Jay Sekulow(757)226-2489), or the National Legal Foundation(757)424-4242, or the American Family Association Law Center (662)844-5036, or the Rutherford Institute (804) 978-3888, and they should be

FLORIDA STATUTE 1006.35

Accuracy of instructional materials.--

(1) In addition to relying on statements of publishers or manufacturers of instructional materials, the commissioner may conduct or cause to be conducted an independent investigation to determine the accuracy of state-adopted instructional materials.

(2) When errors in state-adopted materials are confirmed, the publisher of the materials shall provide to each district school board that has purchased the materials the corrections in a format approved by the commissioner.

(3) The commissioner may remove materials from the list of state-adopted materials if he or she finds that the content is in error and the publisher refuses to correct the error when notified by the department.

(4) The commissioner may remove materials from the list of state-adopted materials at the request of the publisher if, in his or her opinion, there is no material impact on the state's education goals.

Texas Administrative Code
Title 19
Education
§66.66 (I) Instructional materials shall present the most factual information accurately and objectively without editorial opinion or bias by the authors. Theories shall be clearly distinguished from facts and presented in an objective manner.

willing bring it to the courts. See religious freedoms on www.drdino.com for more information.

Two states passed laws **mandating** that the schools teach creation. These laws were ruled unconstitutional. The teachers have always had the right to teach it.

"The Supreme Court decision says only that the Louisiana law violates the constitutional separation of church and state: it does not say that no one can teach scientific creationism — and, unfortunately, many individual teachers do. Some school districts even require 'equal time' for creation and evolution." Eugenie Scott, National Center for Science Education, Berkeley, California, Nature 329, 1987 p. 282

When I speak in public schools, I purposely do not use the Bible or mention God because I do not want to close the door for future ministry. I may demand my rights and lose my opportunity to get anything in the schools. You can get a copy of our video -Public School Presentation and give them to all the teachers in your school.

12. Q: What can public school kids and their parents do about evolution being taught in the public school system?

A: Here are some practical suggestions students and their parents can use to fight evolution in the classroom. It certainly is unfair to use tax dollars to promote the religion of evolution and, at the same time, destroy the faith of Christian children in school.

Parents:

• Transfer your child from public school to private or home school. Public schools lose funding when enrollment drops. See www.exodusmandate.org.

• As a taxpayer, you have a right to help control your local schools, even if your children do not attend. Go to school board meetings.

• Lobby for a law requiring a warning sticker in every book that contains evolution. Stephanie Bell, (334) 272-2777, implemented such a warning sticker law for Alabama textbooks.

• Write to textbook publishers to express your opinion.

• Run for school board or get on your textbook selection committee and demand that books be accurate. Most states already have laws requiring this. Getting false information out of the books will remove many items currently used to support evolution. See my Are You Being Brainwashed by Your Public School Textbook? for more on this topic, or my seminar video #4. Twenty-two of the 50 states have a state textbook selection committee. (In the other states the local district or the individual teachers will chose which books they

This sticker is required to be in all textbooks:

A message from the Alabama State Board of Education.

This textbook discusses evolution, a controversial theory some scientists present as a scientific explanation for the origin of living things, such as plants, animals and humans.

No one was present when life first appeared on earth. Therefore, any statement about life's origins should be considered as theory, not fact.

The word "evolution" may refer to many types of change. Evolution describes changes that occur within a species. (White moths, for example, may "evolve" into gray moths.) This process is microevolution, which can be observed and described as fact. Evoultion may also refer to the change of one living thing to another, such as reptiles into bitds. This process, called macroevolution, has never been observed and should be considered a theory. Evolution also refers to the unproven belief that random, undirected forces produced a world of living things.

There are many unanswered questions about the origin of life which are not mentioned in your textbook, including:
— Why did the major groups of animals suddenly appear in the fossil record (known as the "Cambrian Explosion")?
— Why have no new major groups of living things appeared in the fossil record for a long time?
— Why do major groups of plants and animals have no transitional forms in the fossil record?
— How did you and all living things come to possess such a complete and complex set of "Instructions" for building a living body?

will buy.) The committee normally selects 4 or 5 books from the 15 or so publishers who may submit books for review. These books are considered state approved and the districts must chose from those books if they want the state to pay for them. Publishers want to sell books so they produce what people will buy. If you chose the least poisonous book of the ones available be sure to write the other publishers and tell them why you did not chose theirs. The Gablers, (903) 753-5993, can be a great help in choosing good books.

- Encourage students to do papers showing the religious nature of evolutionary theory in science class. Your school board may be persuaded to buy some material for the sake of equal time. If not, get and distribute books and videos as a mission project through your church.

- Donate Creation Science tapes to your child's science teacher or school library.

- Inform teachers of their right to teach creation in public school. Many are fooled by the propaganda from groups like the ACLU into thinking they are not allowed to talk about creation when they really are.

(See Impact article # 196 from Institute for Creation Research (619) 448-0900 or Teaching Creation Science in the Public School by Duane Gish available from CSE - $4.75)

Keep informed of trends in education and bills being introduced by getting on "the loop." Contact Fred at Fredb001@spectra.net.

Students:

- Earn good grades; behave well; be on time; be respectful.

- Pray for your teacher.

- Talk to your teacher about evolution and creation issues privately, after class. Try to not confront them in class, if possible.

- Offer your teacher creation science material to read or watch. A video is a great non-offensive way to convert teachers to the truths of creation. (Seminar part 1 or 4 would be good.)

- Have your parents demand that you be exempted from the evolutionary portions of class as they are contrary to your religion. (See Students' Legal Rights on a Public School Campus by J. W. Brinkley or Students' Rights in Public Education by the Rutherford Institute. Both available from CSE)

"The battle for humankind's future must be waged and won in the public school classroom by teachers who correctly percieve their role as the proselytizers of a new faith: A religion of humanity...utilizing a classroom instead of a pulpit to carry humanist values into wherever they teach.... The classroom must and will become an arena of conflict between the old and the new—the rotting corpse of Christianity, together with its adjacent evils and misery, and the new faith of humanism...."
—**John J. Dunphy,** Prize-winning Essay, *The Humanist,* Jan/Feb 1983

"Great spirits have always encountered violent opposition from mediocre minds."
—**Albert Einstein**

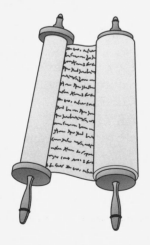

Bible Questions:

13. Q: Are there contradictions in the Bible?

A: When I was a new Christian, someone showed me the apparent contradictions between the creation accounts in Genesis 1 and Genesis 2. According to Genesis 1, God made the trees on day three, the birds from water on day five, and the animals on day six, all before man. But Genesis 2 records the creation of trees, animals, and birds from dirt on day six, all after man. This apparent contradiction disappears when one reads in Genesis 2 that this chapter describes the events regarding the creation of the items in the Garden of Eden only. God knew Satan could come and say he had created all things if Adam did not actually witness God's creative power. God made Adam on the sixth day, put him in the garden, made some trees to grow before Adam, then made 1 more of each of the animals so that Adam could name them and select a wife. The rest of the world was already full of plants and animals from earlier in the week. See p.35

Another apparent contradiction appears in I Kings 7:23 and II Chronicles 4, the description of the large bowl called the brazen laver. According to both passages, the laver measures 10 cubits (elbow to fingertip, about 18 inches) across and 30 cubits around, a ratio that does not equal pi (3.14159…) and appears to be not mathematically valid. However, the 10 cubit measurement spans the inside of the bowl; the handbreadth thickness of the brass is included in the diameter which balances the ratio to equal pi very neatly. There are no contradictions in the Bible. This topic is covered in more detail with pictures and calculations early in the seminar notebook on p.34

Some have supposed a contradiction over the number of horses Solomon had. "And Solomon had forty thousand stalls of horses and chariots, and twelve thousand horsemen." I Kings 4:26, vs. "And Solomon had four thousand stalls for horses and chariots, and twelve thousand horsemen;" II Chronicles 9:25. This is not a problem. One passage tells of the number of horses while the other tells of the number of stalls for horses and chariots. They had ten horses and ten men per chariot. The same ratio is seen in II Samuel 10:18, "And the Syrians fled before Israel; and David slew the men of seven hundred chariots of the Syrians," I Chronicles 19:18. "But the Syrians fled before Israel; and David slew of the Syrians seven thousand men which fought in chariots," See also: II Samuel 8:4, I Chronicles 18:4.

Another common contradiction pointed out by scoffers is, "And those that died in the plague were twenty and four thousand." Numbers 25:9. vs. "Neither let us commit fornication, as some of them committed, and fell in one day three and

and twenty thousand." I Cor. 10:8. Obviously, one thousand died later from the plague.

The Bible Baptist Bookstore in Pensacola, (850) 476-2945, has a great book (even though the author is a little sarcastic with his response to the scoffers questions) dealing with all of the other so-called contradictions or problem passages in the Bible. The book is called Problem Texts and costs about $15

14. Q: Where did the races come from?

A: Actually, there is only one race; the human race. Obviously, several different colors of people exist on the earth that have distinctive characteristics, but they are the same race. Because Scripture does not state where these differences came from, I'm not going to be dogmatic but I will tell you about the various theories.

One theory says that Adam and Eve were medium-brown, possibly because they were made from the earth. That medium-brown couple produced all the varieties of colors; they might have had 100 children or more with all the colors represented in the first family.

A second theory says that the first division of colors came when God put a mark upon Cain (Genesis 4:15) after Cain killed Abel. The Bible doesn't say what the mark is, but some have tried to say that Cain became the first black man. Of course, that theory only explains two colors and does not consider the flood bringing the human race back to one family I personally don't believe this theory either.

A third theory says that Noah cursed Canaan after Noah got drunk (Genesis 9:25). Some people think Canaan became the first black man. I don't believe this theory because I don't think any color of people are cursed and it only explains two colors. The Bible says Canaan shall be a servant of servants. Many have used this verse with their twisted logic to justify slavery.

The fourth (and I think the best) theory says the races came from the Tower of Babel. Genesis 10:20 says, "These are the sons of Ham, after their families, after their tongues, in their countries, in their nations." Perhaps all families, countries, nations, and tongues were created or developed from this event. Maybe the colors were divinely created at that time, or maybe they are just a natural product of a small group of people speaking their own language and marrying back to their own parent stock. Racial traits become more pronounced in a small inbreeding group. The Bible isn't clear on this subject. These four theories are the only ones that I know. I prefer the Tower of Babel explanation. I know the Bible does say in Acts 17 that all nations are of one blood so there is no reason for anyone to be a racist.

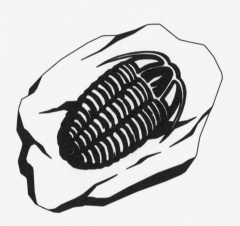

"In this world, if a man sits down to think, he is immediately asked if he has a headache."
—Ralph Waldo Emerson

"Our enemy is not those with guns, but missionaries with Bibles."
—Jiang Zhernin, head of the Communist Party, Peoples Republic of China.

Gulf of Aqaba

"When you come to a fork in the road, take it."
—Yogi Berra

"Professor Alfredo Trombetti claims that he can prove the common origin of all languages. Max Mueller, one of the greatest oriental language scholars, declared that all human languages can be traced back to one, single original language."
—Grant R. Jeffrey, *The Signature of God*

"The true test of civilization is, not the census, nor the size of cities, nor the crops—no, but the kind of man the country turns out.."
—Ralph Waldo Emerson

15. Q: Is there any scientific explanation for the opening of the Red Sea and Moses leading the children of Israel across the bottom?

A: I don't know of any scientific explanation at all, I would say it had to be a miracle. There is, however, archaeological support for the Biblical account. Archaeologists have been looking in the wrong place for the last 3,000 years for the remains of Pharaoh's army at the Red Sea crossing. If you look at a map of the north end of the Red Sea you will see that it splits into two branches. The left branch is called the Gulf of Suez and the right branch is called the Gulf of Aqaba: The children of Israel did not cross at the Gulf of Suez. They traveled across the Sinai Peninsula and crossed over at the Gulf of Aqaba, which is also part of the Red Sea.

Ron Wyatt, (deceased) was a friend of mine from Nashville, Tennessee, researched the crossing of the Red Sea: He found two stone pillars, one on either side of the Gulf of Aqaba, erected and inscribed by Solomon to commemorate the Red Sea crossing. Across the bottom of the gulf between the two pillars is a path littered with the remains of gold-plated wooden chariots and chariot wheels not attached to their chariots, just as the Bible says in Exodus 14:25. God performed a miracle at the Red Sea, and there is evidence of the miracle. Ron's ministry, www.wyattmuseum.com, has a great video on this topic.

16. Q: Is God getting old?

A: This is an interesting question that reflects a common human tendency. People often try to put our human limitations on God. The God of the Bible does not have our limitations. It is difficult to comprehend God as not being affected by time, space or matter like we are. There is a story that may help explain how God is beyond understanding. Suppose there were two flat people represented by two rectangular pieces of paper. These flat people lived on a tabletop. We will call them Mr. Flat and Mrs. Flat and the place they live in and understand is called Flatland. They are two-dimensional beings and live in a two dimensional world. They have no concept of the third dimension. They can see only one dimension (width) but they can perceive two, length and width; just as humans can see two dimensions, length and width and perceive a third, depth. (Hence, the term "depth perception.")

Now suppose that a three-dimensional being (a human) wished to meet and explain himself to Mr. and Mrs. Flat. If that person stuck a finger through the table top called Flatland, Mr. and Mrs. Flat would see only a circle, (the cross section of the finger) with no perception of the rest of the person. Three dimensions are beyond their comprehension in

"Wherefore God also gave them up to uncleanness through the lusts of their own hearts, to dishonour their own bodies between themselves: Who changed the truth of God into a lie, and worshipped and served the creature more than the Creator, who is blessed for ever. Amen."
—**Romans 1:24-25**

"The great difference between the real statesman and the pretender is, that the one sees into the future, while the other regards only the present; the one lives by the day, and acts on expediency; the other acts on enduring principles and for immortality."
—**Edmund Burke**

the same way God is beyond our comprehension. Ephesians 3:18-19 says, "May be able to comprehend with all saints what is breadth, and length, and depth, and height; (four dimensions) And to know the love of Christ, which passeth knowledge, that ye might be filled with all the fullness of God." God may exist in more dimensions than we can fully comprehend now. When we ask a question like "is God getting old," we assume that God exists in time like we do. He does not. He exists beyond time, space, and matter; humans are the ones stuck in time. So God does not grow old. Time, space and matter do not apply to Him or affect Him in any way. He created them all in Genesis 1:1.

17. Q: When were angels created?

A: The Bible says in Exodus 20:11 that God made everything in those six days, heaven and earth and everything in them. The angles had to be made during the first six days, although the Bible doesn't state when. Several references seem to say that the angels rejoiced when the earth's foundations were laid, they must have been created early in the week. See Job 38:4-7. This passage may be referring to the angels watching the dry land appear on day three in the original creation or it may be they were watching the establishing of the earth's new continental levels after the flood. I don't know for sure.

18. Q: What are unicorns?

A: I've never found a good answer to that one. The Bible mentions this creature six times in Numbers 23:22, 24:8, Job 39:9-10, Psalms 29:6, 92:10. I suspect all the pictures of horses with horns have been so imbedded in our minds we cannot get them out. Scripture mentions the unicorn's great strength, aversion to man, and un-trainability. Horses are domestic animals that train well; reptiles are wild animals with small brains that don't train well, if at all. If we could start fresh and read what the Bible says about unicorns, I think we would find that a stocky strong reptile like the triceratops or monoclonius would fit the description much better. We have all seen so many pictures of a horse with a horn that I doubt we will be able to clear our minds and think about this subject without bias. We will have to wait and ask God that question.

19. Q: When did Satan fall from Heaven?

A: I believe the Genesis account is to be taken literally just as it was written. It teaches the world was created in six, twenty-four hour days about 6000 years ago; there was no gap. There was no period of time before the original creation. There was actually no time. God made time as well as matter and space. I Do not think that Satan fell from heaven until about one hundred years after the creation. He could not have fallen

"Will the unicorn be willing to serve thee, or abide by thy crib?
Canst thou bind the unicorn with his band in the furrow? or will he harrow the valleys after thee?"
—Job 39:9-10

before the creation because he was spoken about in the book of Ezekiel as being good while in the garden. Look at Ezekiel 28:13-15, "Thou hast been in Eden the garden of God; every precious stone was thy covering, the sardius, topaz, and the diamond, the beryl, the onyx, and the jasper, the sapphire, the emerald, and the carbuncle, and gold: the workmanship of thy tabrets and of thy pipes was prepared in thee in the day that thou wast created. Thou art the anointed cherub that covereth; and I have set thee so: thou wast upon the holy mountain of God; thou hast walked up and down in the midst of the stones of fire. Thou wast perfect in thy ways from the day that thou wast created, till iniquity was found in thee." He was Lucifer, a good angel, or cherub, and he was in the Garden. The Garden of Eden wasn't made until day six, so that shoots the Gap Theory full of holes right there. Not only that, but Jesus said in Matthew 19:4 that the creation of Adam and Eve was the beginning. Read what it says: "And he answered and said unto them, Have ye not read, that he which made them at the beginning made them male and female." Romans 5:12 says that there was no death until Adam sinned, "Wherefore, as by one man sin entered into the world, and death by sin; and so death passed upon all men, for that all have sinned." Those who say that Satan fell from heaven and wiped out the preadamic civilization are placing death before sin. They have just eliminated the need for Christ to die on the cross. There was no death until sin came into the world. Exodus 20:11 states, "For in six days the LORD made heaven and earth and all that in them is..." This is found in the middle of the ten commandments.

God made the whole universe in six, literal twenty-four hour days, including time, including the angels, and everything that is. What day He made the angels is not known since the Genesis story is mainly telling events on the earth. The angels were probably made on the first day, before God laid the foundations of the earth (see Job 38:4-7 and Gen 1:9). Genesis 1:31 tells us everything was very good at the end of the creation week, so Satan had not fallen yet. Satan did not fall until after the creation, maybe even one hundred or so years later. All that we know is Adam was one hundred thirty when Seth was born. That is the first date given in Scripture. Before Seth, they had Cain and Abel, but dates are not given. Before he had Cain and Abel, they were removed from the garden. Therefore, it would have been somewhere around a hundred years during which time Satan may have become jealous of the fellowship that Adam and Eve enjoyed with God. Satan may have observed their relationship for one hundred years, and said, "Hey, I want them to worship me! I want to rule humanity. I want to walk with them in the garden. I will ascend unto the high heavens. I will take over the seat of the Most High. I will, I will, I will." (See Isaiah 14)

that Satan did not fall until one hundred years after the creation. The fall could not have been in the original creation because he was still the light bearer in the Garden of Eden. See seminar #2 for more information on this topic.

20. Q: How old was Terah when Abram was born 70 or 130?

A: This is an interesting question. Compare the following verses: Gen. 11:26 "And Terah lived seventy years, and begat Abram, Nahor, and Haran." Gen. 12:4 "So Abram departed, as the LORD had spoken unto him; and Lot went with him: and Abram was seventy and five years old when he departed out of Haran." Acts 7:2-4 says "And he said, Men, brethren, and fathers, hearken; The God of glory appeared unto our father Abraham, when he was in Mesopotamia, before he dwelt in Charran, And said unto him, Get thee out of thy country and from thy kindred, and come into the land which I shall show thee. Then came he out of the land of the Chaldaeans, and dwelt in Charran: and from thence, when his father was dead, he removed him into this land, wherein ye now dwell."

The book of Jasher (mentioned in Joshua 10:13 and II Sam. 1:18) is not inspired scripture but it is interesting ancient history. It tells us:

Jasher 12:61 "And Abram hastened and ran to safety to the house of Noah and his son Shem...69. and Abram ceased to speak when Noah and his son Shem answered Terah...

13:1. And Terah took his son Abram and his grandson Lot, the son of Haran, and Sarai his daughter-in-law, the wife of his son Abram, and all the souls of his household and went with them from Ur Casdim to go to the land of Canaan. And when they came as far as the land of Haran they remained there, for it was exceedingly good land for pasture, and of sufficient extend for those who accompanied them.

2. And the people of the land of Haran saw that Abram was good and upright with God and men, and that the Lord his God was with him, and some of the people of the land of Haran came and joined Abram, and he taught them the instruction of the Lord and his ways; and these men remained with Abram in his house and they adhered to him.

3. And Abram remained in the land three years, and at the expiration of three years the Lord appeared to Abram and said unto him; I am the Lord who brought thee forth from Ur Casdim, and delivered thee from the hands of all thine enemies.

4. And now therefore if thou wilt harken to my voice and keep my commandments, my statutes and my laws, then will I cause thy enemies to fall before thee, and I will multiply thy seed like the stars of heaven, and I will send my blessing upon all the works of thy hands, and thou shalt lack nothing.

5. Arise now, take thy wife and all belonging to thee and go to

"The rocks do date the fossils, but the fossils date the rocks more accurately. Stratigraphy cannot avoid this kind of reasoning if it insists on using only temporal concepts, because circularity is inherent in the derivation of time scales." **—O'Rourke, J. E.,** "Pragmatism versus Materialism in Stratigraphy," *American Journal of Science*, vol. 276 (January 1976), p. 53

"Radiometric dating would not have been feasible if the geologic column had not been erected first."
—O'Rourke, J. E., "Pragmatism versus Materialism in Stratigraphy," *American Journal of Science*, vol. 276 (January,1976), p. 54.

"Long regarded as a vestigial organ with no function in the human body, the appendix is now thought to be one of the sites where immune responses are initiated."
—Roy Hartenstein, *Grolier Encyclopedia, 1998.*

the land of Canaan and remain there, and I will there be unto thee for a God, and I will bless thee. And Abram rose and took his wife and all belonging to him, and he went to the land of Canaan as the Lord had told him; and Abram was fifty years old when he went from Haran.

6. And Abram came to the land of Canaan and dwelt in the midst of the city, and he there pitched his tent amongst the children of Canaan, inhabitants of the land.

7. And the Lord appeared to Abram when he came to the land of Canaan, and said to him, This is the land which I gave unto thee and to thy seed after thee forever, and I will make thy seed like the starts of heaven, and I will give unto thy seed for an inheritance all the lands which thou seest.

8. And Abram built an altar in the place where God had spoken to him, and Abram there called upon the name of the Lord.

9. At that time, at the end of three years of Abram's dwelling in the land of Canaan, in the year Noah died, which was the fifty-eighth year of the life of Abram; and all the days that Noah lived were nine hundred and fifty years and he died.

10. And Abram dwelt in the land of Canaan, he, his wife, and all belonging to him, together with those that joined him from the people of the land; but Nahor, Abram's brother, and Terah his father, and Lot the son of Haran and all belonging to them dwelt in Haran.

Solution: There are several possible answers to this question. 1. Some think Abram was not the first born even though his name appears first. The same thing happens with Shem, Ham and Japheth even though Japheth is the elder (Gen. 5:32). 2. Abram made several trips to and from Haran so Terah was 70 when Abram was born. 3. Acts 7:4 refers to Abram taking the body of Terah from Haran to Canaan. Our chart shows Terah at 70 when Abram was born though the scripture does not seem to give enough detail to be dogmatic.

Flood Questions:

21. Q: Did it rain before the flood?

A: The Bible teaches that before the flood a canopy of water surrounded the earth. This canopy is mentioned in Gen. 1:6&7 and II Peter 3:5. The Creation account in Genesis 1 records that a mist that went forth and watered the face of the whole ground. Genesis mentions no other precipitation until the flood brought rain for 40 days and 40 nights. Many people teach that rain never fell before the flood. Although that is probably true, it cannot be taught dogmatically because the Bible simply does not mention the subject. Possibly if the canopy of water that is mentioned in Genesis 1:6 and 7 increased the air pressure, as many think it did, rain was not possible.

"Origin of Species Not addressed in 1859, and is still a mystery in 1998... Both the origin of life and the origin of the major groups of animals remains unknown."
—Alfred G. Fisher,
evolutionist Grolier Multimedia Encyclopedia 1998, fossil section

"Of fowls after their kind, and of cattle after their kind, of every creeping thing of the earth after his kind, two of every sort shall come unto thee, to keep them alive."
—Genesis 6:20

It may be that Noah was preaching that rain would come out of the sky (something that had never happened), and the people laughed just like today when Christians preach that Jesus will come out of the sky (something that has never happened) to catch up all believers in Christ. See Matthew 24:37, Luke 17:26 and I Thess 4:16.

22. Q: How did Noah take care of all those animals on the ark?

A: It is reasonable to assume that all types of animals on the Ark were young animals because they would weigh less, eat less, and sleep more. Many animals become dormant, lethargic or even hibernate during stormy weather. Also, after the flood they would live longer to produce more offspring. No one knows for sure how many animals were on the ark. Limiting it down to two of each **kind** does not mean there were two of each **species** or variety that we have today. There seem to be about 8000 basic kinds of animal in the world.

Through the instructions that God gave or through the wisdom of Noah he was given the ability to provide a watering mechanism to disperse water to the animals throughout the ark and possibly even a food distribution system. In Genesis 1:29-30, the Bible teaches that before the flood all the animals were vegetarians so there was not a problem with, for example, the lion trying to eat the lamb. Some have suggested that there was a moon pool, a hole in the center of the floor, which would provide a place for fishing and, if necessary, a way to dispense animal waste from the ark. See video #3 for more on this topic.

The minor problems that the Bible believers cannot always answer are nothing compared to the problems and questions that the evolutionists cannot answer. Although I do not know exactly how Noah took care of all the animals on the ark, I am going to believe the Bible until it is proven wrong instead of doubt the Bible until it is proven right. For someone to reject the Bible and then accept the story that we all came from a rock is silly!

23. Q: Did Noah have to take all the millions of species of insects on the Ark?

A: Noah was commanded to take into the Ark all the animals on land in whose nostrils was the breath of life (Genesis 6:17, 7:14-15, 22). I do not believe that all the varieties of insects were on the Ark because they breathe through their skin and do not have nostrils. They could have survived on floating matter or by burrowing in the mud. Some of the insects may have been on the Ark in the fur of the animals or in nooks and crannies of the ark; the Bible does not teach that they had to be on board.

"To suppose that the eye...could have been formed by natural selection, seems, I freely confess, absurd in the highest degree."
—**Charles Darwin**
The Origin of Species by Means of Natural Selection or The Preservation of Favored Races in the Struggle for Life
Charles Darwin 1859 p. 217

All in whose nostrils was the breath of life, of all that was in the dry land,
—Genesis 7:22

And of every living thing of all flesh, two of every sort shalt thou bring into the ark, to keep them alive with thee; they shall be male and female.
—Genesis 6:19

24. Q: How did animals travel from all over the world to get to the Ark?

A: This question assumes that the world before the flood was like the world is today with animals specialized for certain areas. Today the world is 70% water and the oceans separate the continents. Also, some animals only live in a few selected locations. The Bible teaches that before the flood the water was gathered into one place (Genesis 1:9). There was probably one ocean and much more landmass. Also, if the climate was more temperate animals could live in all types of places which means Noah did not have to go gather animals from all over the world. In fact, the Bible says that the animals came to Noah (Genesis 6:20).

25. Q: What about dinosaurs? Did they live with Adam and Eve? Did Noah take them on the ark?

A: The dinosaur question is dealt with for over 2 hours on my video-tape #3 of the creation seminar series. To summarize briefly: Dinosaurs were made the sixth day with the rest of the animals. Noah took them on the ark (probably young ones). They have always lived with man. After the flood many died from the climate changes and from man's hunting. They were called dragons for many centuries. (The word dinosaur was just invented in 1841.) A few small dinosaurs may still be alive today in remote parts of the world. There have been over 20,000 reported sightings of dinosaur like creatures in this century. A few pictures and stories are on my web site.

26. Q: It would take 4.4 billion cubic kilometers of water to cover Mt. Everest. Where did the water come from to flood the earth?

A: This question assumes that the pre-flood world was like the world is today. It would only take one inch of water to cover Mt. Everest if the earth were smooth. The Bible states clearly that the water was 15 cubits over the tallest mountain. Seashell fossils have been found on top of mountain ranges all over the world. The top of Mt. Everest is covered with sedimentary rock containing petrified, closed clams. Since clams open as soon as they die, they had to have been buried alive to be petrified in the closed position. There was definitely a worldwide flood. The Bible says in Psalm 104 that as the flood ended the mountains lifted up and the valleys sank down and the water hasted away. Today's mountain ranges are well above sea level, but this was not the case before the flood. If the earth were smoothed out that is, the mountains pressed down and the ocean basins lifted up, there is enough water in the oceans right now to cover the entire earth 8,000 feet deep (approximately 1½ miles).

All of the water ran off rapidly through the soft sediments

"The first living cells emerged between 4 billion and 3.8 billion years ago. There is no record of the event."
—*Biology: The Unity and diversity of Life* Wadsworth 1992 p. 300

into the ocean basins during the last few months of the flood. This would explain the rapid carving of features such as the Grand Canyon and the Bad Lands. See video #6 for lots more on this.

27. Q: During the flood how did the fresh water fish survive?

A: This question assumes the oceans were salt water during the flood like they are today. I believe the entire world was largely fresh water. Today about 30% of the rain water washes into the oceans, bringing mineral salts with it. The oceans are getting saltier every day. Today's oceans are about 3.6% salt. Between the salts washing in from ground water and the salts leaching in from subterranean salt domes, the oceans could have gone from fresh water to 3.6% in the 4400 years since the flood. If the earth were billions of years old, the oceans would be much saltier – like the Dead Sea or Great Salt Lake.

Many animals have adapted to the slow increase in salinity over the last 4400 years. We now have fresh water crocodiles and salt water crocodiles that are different species but probably had a common ancestor. A crocodile! This is not evolution. It is only variation. Changing from a fresh water croc to a salt-water croc is not a major change compared to what the evolutionists believe. They think it changed from a rock to a croc! That would be a major change!

Several years ago, a man in Minnesota told me that he had two large aquariums in his house, one fresh water and the other salt water. He wondered if he could mix the fish together so he figured out how to slowly raise the salt content in the fresh water aquarium a little each week for 10 years until it was 1.8% salt. At the same time, he was lowering the salt content in the salt water aquarium to 1.8% salt. After 10 years he mixed all the fish together. He told me they adapted fine.

Noah had no problem with drinking water during the flood and the fresh-water/salt-water problem does not exist. Attempting to force the way the world is today onto the questions involving the pre-flood world is a common problem. II Peter 3 says the scoffers of the last days will be willingly ignorant of how God made the heavens and the earth (the original creation), and the flood.

28. Q: If there was really a world wide flood where are all the bones of the humans that drowned?

A: I believe there are few human fossils for several reasons.

1. God made the world full of plants and animals but only two people. 1600 years later the world was still full of plants and animals but still not full of people. There were not as many of them to be drowned.

"In the years after Darwin, his advocates hoped to find predictable progressions. In general, these have not been found—yet the optimism has died hard, and some pure fantasy has crept into textbooks."
—Raup, David M.,
"Evolution and the Fossil Record," *Science*, vol. 213 (July 17, 1981), p. 289

"All those trees of life with their branches of our ancestors, that's a lot of nonsense."
—Mary Leakey,
Associated Press Dec. 10, 1996

2. Men are smarter than animals (that is, some men), so he would figure out a way to avoid drowning until the last possible minute by making makeshift rafts or holding to floating logs and tend to be deposited on top rather than in the sediments. Therefore, he would not fossilize. For example, millions of bison were slaughtered in the west a century ago, yet few, if any, fossilized. They were left on top to rot, bones and all.

3. Since so many researchers have the preconceived (and false) idea that man has been evolving from small and dumb to big and smart they may tend to not even recognize and properly identify bone fragments of humans that may have been huge by today's standards. Their prejudice is that ancient man was smaller. We show evidence for giant humans on video #2.

In spite of the above problems, Marvin Lubenow, an expert on fossil humans and author of Bones of Contention (available from CSE) says that about 4000 human fossil remains have been found.

The evolutionist has a serious problem with this same question. If man has really been here for millions of years there should be many thousands, if not millions, of fossils of their bones like we have of the animals. The "where are the bones?" question is really a question for the evolutionist to answer if he expects all the taxpayers to support his religion in the school system.

Miscellaneous Questions:

29. Q: What is the Gaia Hypothesis?

A: The Gaia hypothesis is named after the Greek goddess for the earth. According to Gaia Hypothesis, earth itself is a living organism, our "Mother Earth," as its proponents call it. Many evolutionists adopt this theory because they have not found any evidence for gradual undirected evolution as Darwin predicted. Radical environmentalism and the New Age Movement tie right into the Gaia Hypothesis and evolution. The Bible teaches the earth was made for man to have dominion over. It is going to be destroyed one day.

30. Q: What about the ozone hole, and R-12 refrigerants?

A: There is not an ozone problem that man has created. Ozone is a natural gas, which is produced when sunlight strikes the atmosphere. O_3, ozone, is poisonous, but it does filter out radiation. In the upper atmosphere, the ozone layer protects us; it's a barrier. Ozone is absent from the North and South Poles because the sun never strikes those areas directly, but at such an oblique angle that it does not produce ozone. It's normal to have an ozone hole in these areas.

"If my theory be true, numberless intermediate varieties... must assuredly have existed;"
—**Charles Darwin,**
The Origin of Species... 1859

"We've got to ride the global warming issue. Even if the theory of global warming is wrong, we will be doing the right things—in terms of economic policy and environmental policy."
—**Timothy Wirth,** Former U.S. Senator (D- Colorado)

"The function of only 1% (some say 3%) of human DNA has been determined. If 99% of this small amount is similar to chimps it still proves nothing."
See: *Modern Creation Trilogy* vol. 2, chapter 9, Henry Morris

What about R-12? R-12 does destroy ozone, but the R-12 from our refrigerators and air conditioners never rises high enough to destroy atmospheric ozone. R-12 sinks; it doesn't rise. Even convection currents would not carry man made R-12 to the ozone layer in 100 years, which is a longer time than man has been using it. Man has done almost nothing to the ozone. In fact, my understanding is that the last time scientists measured the ozone layer, it was thicker than it was the first time they measured it. I believe the real purpose of the environmental propaganda is to fulfill the first plank of the Communist Manifesto: the abolishment of private property. While there is no question man has abused the environment, there is a hidden agenda behind the modern hype. (See Facts Not Fear for information on environment.)

31. Q: What about global warming?

A: Just about as many scientists are concerned about global freezing or another ice age as about global warming. There isn't enough data to be dogmatic. The answer would probably depend upon the grant money being sought. As with the previous question, most of the environmental hype is really to help bring about Karl Marx's dream (nightmare) of a Communist world. His first of 10 planks was the abolishing of private property. Though there are many sincere people in the environmental movement, I believe the real agenda is Communism, not saving the planet.

32. Q: Who built the Great Pyramid, and why?

A: No one knows for sure who built the Great Pyramid, but several theories have been proposed. Some think it is just another of the pyramids built by the Egyptians. Some think Adam and his sons built it before the flood. Some think Enoch built it and that it is the only structure to survive the flood. Others say Noah and his sons built it after the flood. According to some experts, it appears that some of its features indicate that it was intended to be a testimony to God. Adam did not have a Bible so God gave him the gospel story in the stars with the 88 constellations telling the entire gospel story and God's plan for the ages. After the flood Noah still did not have a Bible so God gave him the gospel story in stone.

• The Great Pyramid has no inscription to any Egyptian king.

• It is the earliest and largest of the 67 pyramids found in Egypt. The later pyramids are of lesser quality and are mere copies of the Great Pyramid.

• Inside, there is a broad way that leads to a pit and a narrow way that leads to the King's Chamber. (Sounds like Matthew 7 to me.)

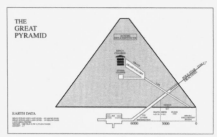

144,000 casing stones- broad way leads to the pit-narrow way leads to kings chamber-90 times the volume of the Sears tower-Top stone never installed.

"The evolutionary trees that adorn our textbooks have data only at the tips and nodes of their branches; the rest is inference, however reasonable, not the evidence of fossils."
—**Stephen Jay Gould,** Harvard University. Evolutions Erratic Pace *Natural History Vol. 5* May 1977

"I fully agree with your comments on the lack of evolutionary transitions in my book. If I knew of any, fossil or living, I would certainly included them. I will lay it on the line—there is not one such fossil..."
—**Dr. Colin Paterson,** Senior Paleontologist, British Museum of Natural History in correspondence to Luther Sunderland quoted in *Darwin's Enigma* 1988 p. 89

• The 153 steps in the pyramid match the 153 fishes gathered in John 21:11, which may be a reference to all nations of the earth gathering into the kingdom of God. (See John 21:11)

• The King's Chamber is on the 50th row of the stones; 50 was the year of Jubilee. (See Lev. 25:11)

• Inside the King's Chamber is a solid carved, empty red granite tomb the same volume as the Ark of the Covenant.

• Although most have been torn off, the pyramid was originally covered with 144,000 polished casing stones, the number of witnesses in Revelation 7. The stones were a perfect fit such that many of the seams could not be seen nor a paper put between them today, thousands of years later.

• The cornerstone at the top is missing, symbolic of Christ, the rejected chief cornerstone (Daniel 2:45; Psalm 118:22; Matthew 21:42; Mk 10:12). The 5 sided cornerstone may represent the number of grace.

• The Great Pyramid is of such magnitude that it could not be built today. It is 90 times the volume of the Chicago Sears Tower. Napoleon said there was enough stone in the pyramid to build a 10 foot high brick wall all the way around France! Some stones near the top, 400 feet from the ground, weigh 70 tons!

• The foundation covers so wide an area (over 13 acres) that it could not be built today as level as it is (less than 1/10 inch error in 13 acres). Every locomotive in the world harnessed to the Pyramid could not pull it The door is so well joined that it was undetectable from the outside for centuries.

• The pyramid sits right on the longest latitude line and the longest longitude line with land above sea level.

• "In that day shall there be an altar to the LORD in the midst of the land of Egypt, and a pillar at the border thereof to the LORD." Is. 19:19. The pyramid is on the border when Egypt was divided into a northern and southern kingdom and in the midst when they united.

• Satan has been using the great pyramid as his symbol for the New World Order. On the back of a $1 bill you will see the pyramid with the all seeing eye (Lucifer) coming down to finish the pyramid. He thinks he will take over God's kingdom, but Jesus will be the one to come to earth and rule and reign for 1000 years. See Rev. 20-22. (See seminar #5 for more.)

33. Q: What is the Bermuda triangle?

A: There are several theories about the Bermuda triangle, some

Natural, some supernatural. Some say it is hype, and nothing happens that does not happen in other parts of the world. The

"After nearly a lifetime of research on the subject, British anatomist and an evolutionist Lord Zuckerman stated that if man evolved from apelike creature there is not even a trace of such evidence in the fossil record."
—**Dr. Duane T. Gish,**
"Evolution, Creation Scientifically Equal"

"Men should not resign his conscience to the legislator... We should be men first and subjects afterward. It is not desirable to cultivate a respect for the law as for the right."
—**Henry David Thoreau**

Bermuda triangle could be a magnetic anomaly resulting from a bending of the earth's magnetic field. There may be a large iron ore deposit or the remnants of an iron meteor buried there that plays havoc with instruments. The ships and planes that report unusual behavior of their instruments may be entering this area of disturbance. Some say the ships are lost due to the violent suction created as the tide goes up and down through the coral reefs there. Small ships have been found down in the deep "blue holes" in the coral. There may be a natural explanation for the reports.

Some have suggested that the triangle is a UFO parking lot, or the entrance to hell. I personally don't believe either of these but I don't have an answer to what is causing the strange happenings there. Although no solid explanation exists, hundreds of reports from reputable people record strange occurrences in the area: A deacon at Wildwood Baptist Church in Oshkosh, Wisconsin gave me a first hand account of his experience while on board a Navy ship in 1962. He was en route to the Cuban missile crisis. As soon as his ship entered the space between Florida, Cuba, and Puerto Rico, everything electrical, including wristwatches and flashlights, quit working. The ship drifted for 24 hours, unable to radio for assistance, until it had left the area and operations suddenly resumed. The area is undoubtedly unusual, although no one that I know understands why. If you can find out please let me know.

34. Q: What about Big-foot?

A: The Big-foot evidence that I have seen relies on eyewitness accounts rather than empirical, scientific evidence. Many people report sightings of creatures with similar descriptions in several countries, as well as over 35 American States. There is no question that many of the sightings are hoaxes, pranks, or mis-identified. These creatures, also called Big-foot, Sasquatch, Yeti, Skunk Ape or the Abominable Snowman, may be an unidentified species of ape. Some have said it is part of a cursed race of humans similar to what happened to Nebuchadnezzar in Daniel 4:33 but those theories are unverified so far. I have personally interviewed 8 people who claim they have seen a Big-foot. Their descriptions agree in many details. They describe it as being like Harry from the movie Harry and the Hendersons. I don't have a good answer to the Big-foot question. I wish I did.

35. Q: What about UFO's?

A: The best information that I have comes from the books and material from Chuck Missler at Koinonia House, PO Box D, Coeur d'Alene, ID 83816, 1-800-khouse1, www.khouse.org or

UFO: End Time Delusion from New Leaf Press, (800) 999-3777, or The Cosmic Conspiracy by Stan Deyo available from www.Amazon.com. According to Deyo, some UFO's are U.S. Government experiments with electrogravitic propulsion as opposed to jet propulsion, while others are Satanic apparitions. For further information, refer to the books. I don't know for sure what they are, but, if I were the Devil and I knew the rapture was coming, I would want to prepare my lie well ahead of time in the minds of the people.

36. Q: Is it possible for your television to watch you?

A: This is just a rumor. There is no evidence that televisions now monitor their viewers, and to my knowledge no technology exists to enable them to do so. It would not surprise me if "big brother" was doing that or working on doing it though. Small cameras could easily be installed in TV's to have them watch you but the picture tube itself cannot do this now. Gary Frye, a good friend of mine, keeps up to date on this type of thing as does Carl Sanders. Gary's # is (704) 782-5273 and Carl's is (870) 269-6113. For years it has been possible to "hot hook" your phone so people can listen to what is being said even if the phone is hung up. Be careful to always tell the truth!

37. Q: What about the Mark of the Beast?

A: Corporations and governments have amazing technology available that has been developed over the last 20 years. Revelation 13:16 says that Satan "causeth all, both small and great, rich and poor, free and bond, to receive a mark." The Greek word translated "mark" literally means "etching." Computer microchips have information etched into silicon. Microchips may play an important part in the mark of the beast.

Many advances have been made in tracking people or items. Microchips can be implanted in pets or cars to track those lost or stolen. Several satellites in earth's orbit can detect the microchip and report its coordinates. Also, Hughes Aircraft Corporation developed a toll booth substitute that tracks cars. As a car passes, this strip in the highway deducts 50 cents (or whatever the toll is) from a debit account, makes an image of the license plate, and checks it to see if the car is registered properly or has been reported stolen and if the driver is wanted by the police. The strip can check eight cars per second at 100 mph per lane. Finally, an imbedded wire along some highways and a new hand-held device both can turn off the ignition of a running car by destroying the car's computer with a burst of energy. These new control and monitoring technologies may be forerunners of the mark of the beast. Dean Martin (dean.l.martin@home.com) has the best seminar I know of on the subject. His phone # is (850) 455-5011. Carl Sanders, P.O. Box 2000, Mountain View, AR 72645, (870) 269-6113, sho-phar@trumpetmin.org, has Great info.

38. Q: How would you answer critics including those who have web sites criticizing you?

A: Amid the hundreds of letters and e-mails we receive each week here at CSE, we occasionally receive one from an atheist, skeptic, critic, scoffer, or even an idiot or two. Several hundred have posted web sites about me. I keep so busy with my hectic travel schedule that I normally do not take time to respond to them in writing more than once. There are so many people who want to hear the truths about creation that it is a waste of time to get distracted answering the scoffers. They will ask hundreds of questions or make hundreds of accusations. I am convinced that most of them don't really want an answer anyway, they want to tie up all my time and prevent the gospel from getting out. If I took the time to answer them all they would only ask a hundred more. We do offer a great book called Creation Scientists Answer their Critics by Dr. Duane Gish that answers many commonly asked questions. I have also produced an audio tape with answers to some of the scoffers' questions and objections. The tape is $3 and can be returned for a full refund. We will add to the tape as time permits. I have a standing offer to face any number of evolutionists at a time in front of their own university, and Dr. Walt Brown has a standing offer to engage qualified scientists in an email debate.

I will be the first to say that I have learned much from my critics and have changed things in my seminars over the years because of their legitimate gripes, corrections and suggestions. "Iron sharpeneth iron." (Prov. 27:17) These critics can be a man's best friend, if they don't distract you from the main job. God knows that I want to be accurate and would never purposely tell a lie to promote my point. I may not always be right, but if I am saying it in my seminar then I don't know it to be false. I work hard and research a lot to try to be right. I am certainly willing to be corrected by friend or foe. Even if it is proven that I am teaching something that is not correct, don't be fooled into thinking that one incorrect statement means everything else I say is wrong. Any third grader should know that.

Evolutionists often try to divert attention from the legitimate points I bring up about their religion. They know their "theory" won't stand close scrutiny so they try to focus people's attention on something else. They will point out a five-second mistake in my 15-hour seminar and assume the entire thing is false. The problems the creationists cannot explain or the unintentional errors in their books or speeches are very minor compared to the mountainous problems the evolutionist is overlooking or ignoring in his own religion. I ask quite a few questions in my seminar notebook and bring up points in my seminar that they seem to conveniently avoid. It doesn't take a rocket scientist to see why they do this.

DR. KURK E. KOCH, Professor, Lectured at 100 Universities in 65 countries on 5 continents. Subjects of expertise: New World Order, Occultism, Extreme Movements, and Parapsychology. His assessment of the coming NWO under the United Nations is that it will reduce everything to one common denominator: "The system will be made up of a single currency, single centrally financed government, single tax system, single language, single political system, single world court of justice, single head (one individual leader), single state religion." He further states: "Each person will have a registered number, without which he will not be allowed to buy or sell; and there will be one universal world church. Anyone who refuses to take part in this universal system will have no right to exist."

The retina of your eye is less than 1 square inch yet contains over 137,000,000 light sensitive cells! How would you like to be the electrician that wired that up!

"He that formed the eye, shall he not see?"
—Psalms 94:8-9

"Scientific naturalists of today will not be convinced by creationist arguments, no matter how persuasive, because their philosophical assumptions prevent it."
—John Weldon, Ph.D.

"It is easy to be conspicuously compassionate if others are being forced to pay the cost."
—M. N. Rothbard

"When the government reduces all of us to the status of a number, that number is going to be zero. With this number no one can ever be lost, but no man can ever again be alone. This is despairing."
—former North Carolina Senator Sam Ervin, in opposition to the Social Security Act.

I confess that I have very little patience with the scoffers after a few exchanges. Maybe it is the Elijah personality in me that wants to mock them as in I Kings 18:27. I am working on trying to be more Christ-like in my dealings with them. I always offer to talk with any skeptic by phone or to debate them publicly, but not in a long drawn out e-mail exchange. They nearly always refuse. Many remain anonymous for some strange reason. I see no reason for this cowardice except maybe Proverbs 28:1 "The wicked flee when no man pursueth: but the righteous are bold as a lion." They do not need to fear me. I will not hurt them. I feel sorry for those whom the Devil has deceived into believing his lies. I will gladly discuss any topic or question with anyone, friend or foe. If I am wrong, I will admit it and change whatever I need to change to make it right. I don't claim to be perfect, and never have, but I serve a God who is and love His Bible, which is perfect.

It is both humorous and sad to see the evolutionists strain so hard at the gnats in the creation theory and then turn around and swallow the camel of evolution. I have read carefully the criticisms of each of these scoffers. Rest assured that my offer to publicly debate any evolutionist (even two or three at a time against just me if that will help) is always open. I do the debates not so much to convert the evolutionist (though I would like to) but because it helps so many in the audience. Most people who have attended or watched my seminar or who have common sense will be able to see through the silly questions the skeptics ask or the ridiculous non-answers they give to my questions. However, if you read the so-called "How Good are those Young Earth Arguments?" by Matson or "300 Creationist Lies" by the cowardly, anonymous "Budikka," or any other of my critics on the web, and something they say raises a question in your mind, please, give me a call. I can defend my position or I will be glad to change. It is a great American tradition that the accused gets to face his accuser. Anonymous critics get little or none of my attention. I travel a lot but we have a very capable staff working at CSE who will answer your questions or leave a message for me with several good times to call you back.

I went through Matson's book and circled every time he used the words "might have," "could have," "scientists believe," etc. His great faith in evolution shows through clearly as his religion, not science. It surprised me how many non-answers they give to the points I raised in my seminar. For example: when answering the problem about the short period comets, Matson said they are being replenished from the Oort Cloud or the Kuiper Belt! No one has ever seen this happen, of course, but he **believes** it to be so. That is an answer based not on science but faith, and he should admit it. The entire answer is filled with typical evolutionist hallucinations. He is always using phrases like "computer simulations," and "theoretical calculations," "would likely," "statistical calculations," "some astronomers estimate," etc. His intention is to show it "could have" happened. Well, I "could have been" president of

"In hope of eternal life, which God, that cannot lie, promised before the world began;"
—Titus 1:2

"And for this cause God shall send them strong delusion, that they should believe a lie: That they all might be damned who believed not the truth, but had pleasure in unrighteousness."
—II Thessalonians. 2:11-12

General Motors, but I'm not! He needs to read, Raymond Littleton, "The Non-existence of the Oort Cometary Shell," Astrophysics and Space Science, Vol. 31 pp. 385-401. There is no Oort cloud.

He concludes his non-answer to the comet question by trying to put the burden on the creationist! He says, "The creationist must prove that there are no reasonable sources for replenishing comets" (p.13). And I say, "No, Dave, if you expect all taxpayers to fund your religion in the public school system, parks, museums, etc., the burden of proof is on you! You may spend **your money** any way you want. You are welcome to believe anything you want and you may teach your children anything you want them to believe; but before you spend **my money** to teach **my children and grandchildren** something I don't want them to believe, the burden of proof is on you!" Shifting the burden of proof is a common tactic to keep an enemy busy. If I said watermelons are blue on the inside until you cut the skin, Prove me wrong! I have shifted the burden on proof on you. That is what most scoffers try to do with their criticisms of creationists. Don't be fooled!

After reading through one scoffer's article called "300 Lies of Creation Scientists," it was hard not to laugh. They sure are getting desperate these days. I told him I don't deal with anonymous cowards, but if he would give me his real name and number, I would be glad to show him when his logic is wrong. He has refused and now is upset because I won't correspond with him any more. I don't waste a lot of time on scoffers because there are so many sincere people who want and need the truth that it is unfair to divert much energy to those who do not want to hear. During the war for states' rights, President Lincoln was getting lots of critical letters. One of his aids asked him if he intended to answer them. Lincoln replied that if he answered all his critics that would absorb all his time and he had a war to win. Nehemiah did the same thing when his enemies wanted him to stop the work and come down to talk about the wall he was building. His answer was classic. Nehemiah 6:3-4 says: "And I sent messengers unto them (his critics), saying, I am doing a great work, so that I cannot come down: why should the work cease, whilst I leave it, and come down to you? Yet they sent unto me four times after this sort; and I answered them after the same manner." Nearly every day a skeptic or scoffer will try to engage me in a letter writing battle via e-mail or standard mail over the creation subject. I have a standing offer of $250,000 for proof for evolution and I stand ready to debate any two or three evolutionists at a time in a public setting, but I won't waste the time to slowly hunt and peck out endless answers when they don't really want one. That would be casting my pearls before swine (see Matthew 7:6). If they are so sure they are right, they should be delighted with the opportunity to debate me publicly. I will even draw the crowd for them!

Atheists seem to have nothing else to do. They know they

"The American people are so enamored by equality that they would rather be equal in slavery than unequal in freedom."
—Alexis de Tocqueville

can't get a crowd together for an atheists' meeting, so they ride on the coattails of the creationists. For example, I recently was invited by the free-thought club on the Ohio State University campus to debate the editor of the American Atheist Magazine. They told me they normally had about 30 people come to their meetings (in a university of 58,000), but they had nearly 90 come when this man spoke the month before. They were proud to tell me about this great attendance! The night of the debate there were hundreds there (several people said there were over 700) to hear the debate. I speak to crowds of over 1000 nearly every week out of the year. The atheists of course have a "smarter than thou" attitude about it all. They say their crowds are small because there are not very many smart people (meaning themselves, of course) in the world. What egos!

If these critics would devote even 5% of their error-detecting attention to the evolution theory like they do to the creation theory, they would see the lies, wild exaggerations and distortions used to support the silly idea that we all came from a rock over the last 4.6 billion years! Converted evolutionists make great creationists. Christians and creationists need to work to be accurate, of course, at the same time we need to realize the evolutionists are not the enemy, Satan is the enemy. It may be hard at times, but we need to love the sinner while we hate the sin. God is not willing that any should perish but that all come to the knowledge of the truth.

40. Q: Where did you get your degree?

A: Every once in a while someone will ask me the question, "Where did you get your degree?" There are many web sites that attack me and often publish false information about me and/or my degree. While I am not the least bit ashamed of my education, I have learned by experience that some are asking the question because they have come to the point where they cannot attack the message I bring against evolution so they wish to attack me personally instead. This is called an ad hominem argument. They mistakenly think that by belittling the man they have answered his points and won the debate. When the opponent in a debate begins using ad hominem attacks, it is an obvious signal to all that they are losing the debate on facts and must resort to other means to try to save face or divert attention. It is also interesting to watch how the evolutionists will spend much time and effort scrutinizing a subject like my degree or credentials yet won't spend two seconds scrutinizing how ridiculous the entire evolution theory is! They truly strain at a gnat and swallow a camel as Jesus said in Matthew 23:24. Two misguided individuals are even writing to every church on my itinerary trying to get the pastors to cancel my meetings! No meetings have been canceled, but several pastors have called me to have a Good laugh over these letters. It is obvious that these critics are unable to get a crowd to voluntarily listen to them preach the evolution religion so they spend time attacking creationists.

"The evolutionary trees that adorn our textbooks have data only at the tips and nodes of their branches; the rest is inference, however reasonable, not the evidence of fossils."
—Stephen Jay Gould, Professor of Geology and Paleontology, Harvard University in "Evolution's Erratic Pace," Natural History, vol. 86 (May, 1977), p. 14

"We should all be concerned with the future because we will have to spend the rest of our lives there."
—Charles F. Kettering

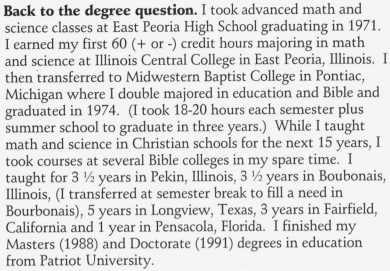

Back to the degree question. I took advanced math and science classes at East Peoria High School graduating in 1971. I earned my first 60 (+ or -) credit hours majoring in math and science at Illinois Central College in East Peoria, Illinois. I then transferred to Midwestern Baptist College in Pontiac, Michigan where I double majored in education and Bible and graduated in 1974. (I took 18-20 hours each semester plus summer school to graduate in three years.) While I taught math and science in Christian schools for the next 15 years, I took courses at several Bible colleges in my spare time. I taught for 3 ½ years in Pekin, Illinois, 3 ½ years in Boubonais, Illinois, (I transferred at semester break to fill a need in Bourbonais), 5 years in Longview, Texas, 3 years in Fairfield, California and 1 year in Pensacola, Florida. I finished my Masters (1988) and Doctorate (1991) degrees in education from Patriot University.

Patriot University www.patriotuniversity.com is a Christian university in Colorado Springs that offers an external studies program for people involved in full time ministries. Patriot University (established 1980) is an extension of Hilltop Baptist Church and offered a Ph.D. in education. I spent many years working on my degree and learned a lot - as anyone who has watched my debates with evolutionists or seminar series will testify. Long after I graduated, Patriot relocated its extension division offices to College Heights Baptist Church in Alamosa, CO where it continues to thrive today. Patriot now offers a Doctor of Ministry degree rather than a Ph.D. in education because the State of Colorado asked them to make the change to emphasize the religious nature of their institution. Some ill informed scoffers have even circulated a picture of the church parsonage next to the church (which has the same address) and claimed this is where Patriot is now located. I don't understand their twisted logic but, evidently, they think this somehow discredits me.

Patriot allows students to give offerings to the school instead of a regular tuition payment. Some scoffers have laughed at this idea; yet, they don't seem to realize this is God's method and they also forget how many thousands have gone through secular schools without using any of their own money via grants, scholarships or their parents' savings.

Some have ridiculed the size of the school. It would be interesting to see the look on the scoffer's face if they knew the size of the schools many of our early presidents, congressmen, and military leaders graduated from. If Harvard offers a Ph.D. degree program with only three or four students (this happens at many schools, sometimes with only one student), does the small number automatically mean they are not "earning their degree" or that they are attending a "diploma mill" school? Of course not! Hundreds of colleges and universities offer classes by correspondence. There is nothing wrong with this. I worked very hard for my degrees. I don't know if others do or not. Patriot has about 25 graduates each year, three to five of which are getting doctorate degrees.

"What is the use of being elected or re-elected unless you stand for something?"
—President Grover Cleveland

"For whosoever shall call upon the name of the Lord shall be saved."
—Romans 10:13

My 20-year study of the creation evolutionism subject led me to start Creation Science Evangelism in 1991. I now speak over 700 times each year on the subject. I have had more than 60 debates and have been a guest on over 4000 radio and television talk shows. My itinerary is available from my office or on my web site, and any evolutionist interested in a public debate is welcome to contact me to arrange a time while I am in their area to be held at a place of their choosing. See my web site for details. Since some seem to think I don't have a "legitimate degree," they can call me Kent, Mr. Hovind or even "hey you," if it will make them feel better. Since they don't think I am "properly educated," it should be easy for them to demonstrate how wrong I am and how much evidence there is for evolution. I should be a pushover, but I am willing to debate them anyway and run the risk of publicly embarrassing myself. BTW, we have now upped our offer to $250,000 for evidence for evolution.

If you would like the names of scientists who support the young earth creationist position you may want to contact the Institute for Creation Research at 619-448-0900 or ICR.ORG. They can supply you with a list. I only claim to have many years of experience in studying the subject and the common sense to know that the universe is too complex to have happened without an incredibly smart designer (whom I happen to know personally as my savior). By the way, Darwin's only degree was in theology; yet, he is often called a great scientist in textbooks today. Who and what determines who gets to be called a "scientist" and why don't these scoffers put the same effort into correcting textbooks that call "Reverend" Darwin a scientist?

As Henry Morris has pointed out, "It is worth noting that almost none of the leaders of this evolutionary revival had been trained as scientists in the modern sense. None were educated as physicists or chemists or biologists or geologists or astronomers or other "natural" scientists. As already noted, Charles Darwin himself was an apostate divinity student whose only degree was in theology. Charles Lyell was a lawyer; William Smith a surveyor, James Hutton an agriculturalist, John Playfair a mathematician, and Robert Chambers a journalist. Alfred Russell Wallace had little formal education of any kind, with only a brief apprenticeship in surveying. Thomas Huxley had an indifferent education in medicine. Herbert Spencer received practically no formal education except some practical experience in railroad engineering. Thomas Malthus was a theologian and economist, while Erasmus Darwin was a medical doctor and poet. Of all the chief contributors to the revival of evolutionism commonly associated with Charles Darwin, only Jean Lamarck in France and Ernst Haeckel in Germany seemed to have had a bona fide education in the branch of evolutionary "science" that they pursued, and they had their own particular anti-Christian agendas to promote." The Long War Against God ch.4. Haeckel and Lamarck pushed wildly wrong ideas to support evolution.

REFERENCE LIST

Study to shew thyself approved unto God,
a workman that needeth not to be ashamed,
rightly divided the word of truth.
— II Timothy 2:15

Sources for more Information:

We try to keep all our information as current as possible. However, addresses, phone numbers, web sites, etc. change from time to time. Therefore, we cannot guarantee the absolute accuracy of all those listed. If you notice something that needs to be changed, please notify us so that corrections might be made before the next edition. Thank you.

American Portrait Films
P.O. Box 19266 • Cleveland, Ohio 44119
(800) 736-4567 • (216) 531-8600
fax (216) 531-8355 • www.amport.com
Good films for families

Answers in Genesis
Ken Ham • P.O. Box 6330
Florence, Kentucky 41042 • (800) 350-3232
www.answersingenesis.org
Creation Magazine

Center for Scientific Creation
Dr. Walter T. Brown, Jr. • 5612 North 20 Place
Phoenix, Arizona 85016 • (602) 955-7663
www.creationscience.com

Common Sense for Today
Don Boys, Ph.D. • P.O. Box 944
Ringold, Georgia 30736 • (706) 965-5930
Dboys@aol.com

Concerned Women for America
Dr. Beverly LaHaye • 1015 Fifteenth St., NW
Suit 1100 Washington, DC 20005
(800) 458-8797
(202) 488-7000 • www.cwfa.org
Radio program and newsletter for the family

Coral Ridge Ministries
Dr. D. James Kennedy • P.O. Box 40
Ft. Lauderdale, FL 33302
(954) 771-8840 • www.coralridge.org
TV/radio programs, books, newsletter

Creation Evidence Museum
Dr. Carl Baugh • P.O. Box 309
Glen Rose, Texas 76043 • (254)897-3200
http://home.texoma.net/~linesden/cem/

Creation Resource Foundation
Dennis Peterson • P.O. Box 570
El Dorado, CA 95623
(800)497-1454 • (916)626-4447
www.awesomeworks.com/crf/siteindex.htm

Creation Moments (formerly Bible Science Association)
26219 Fremont Dr • Zimmerman, Minn 55398
(800) 422-4253 • (612) 856-2552
fax (612)856-2525
Great source for books on creation.

Creation Science Association for Mid-America
22509 State Line Road • Cleveland, Missouri 64734 • (816) 618-3610 • www.csama.org

Creation Truth Foundation, Inc.
Dr. G. Thomas Sharp • P.O. Box 1435
Noble, Oklahoma 73068 • (405)872-9856

Institute for Creation Research
P.O. Box 2667 •El Cajon, California 92021
(619)448-0900 • www.icr.org

Marrs, Texe
Living Truth Ministries • 1708 Patterson Road
Austin, Texas 78733 • (800) 234-9673
www.texemarrs.com
Information regarding the New World Order

Master Books
P.O. Box 727 • Green Forest, AR 72638
(800)999-3777

Media Bypass
(800)4-BYPASS • www.4bypass.com
Patriot magazine

Museum of Earth and Life History
Dr. James Hall • Liberty University
Lynchburg, Virginia 24506 • (800) 522-6225

Second Coming Ministry
Terry L. Cook
774 Mays Blvd., Suite 10
Incline Village, Nevada 89451
(775)833-1803
Info on mark of the Beast, implantable biochip, or to schedule his seminar.

Science Frontiers
P.O. Box 107 •
Glen Arm, Maryland 21057

Traditional Values Coalition
Rev. Lou Sheldon • P.O. Box 940
Anaheim, CA 92815 • (714)520-0300

Trumpet Ministries
P.O. Box 2000
Mountain View, AR 72560
(870) 880-6285
www.trumpetmin.org
Sho-phar@trumpetmin.org

Wallbuilders, Inc.
P.O. Box 397 • Aledo, Texas 76008
(800) 873-2845 • (817) 441-6044
www.wallbuilders.com

Washington Times
(202)636-3333 • www.washtimes.com
Newspaper covering stories not found in
liberal media; daily publications can be
mailed to your home

"The Road Called Life"

The road of life, it seems to me, is not as smooth as it should be.
Sometimes the road seems all uphill, like swallowing a bitter pill.
Sometimes the bumps get really rough, and you give up, or else get tough.
But the hardest part, it seems to me, is when you drive up to a "T."

You must go left or else go right, and that's what makes my stomach tight.
Decisions seem so hard to make, but I must choose which road to take.
That choice determines where I'll be and also my whole family.
I asked for help from those around, but their view, too, was from the ground.

And so I asked the One I knew (Who up in heaven has a view),
Of all the roads that I might take, to keep me right for Jesus' sake.
I prayed and prayed and then I chose, and was I right? My Father knows.
But He won't say too much to me; He saves it for eternity.

And then I think that He will say, "My son, you could have chosen either way.
I'm more concerned about your heart, than where you go or when you start.
It's not so much which way you go, but what you do with what you know.
You may go left or right or straight. I'll meet you at the pearly gate.
And welcome you with open arms, and keep you safe from all life's harms."

I s'pose I'll wonder every day, "What if I'd gone the other way?"
But this time I'll just do my best and pack my stuff and head out West.

Written By Dr. Hovind while praying about a major move.

Bibliography: Recommended Reading

Creation Science Evangelism does not necessarily agree with every viewpoint given in each book.

Bible Related

Answer Book, The
Samuel Gipp • DayStar Publications
164 pages • Available from CSE $6.50

Archko Volume, The
Randall Reinstedt • McGraw-Hill
248 pages • Available from CSE $16.50

Language of the King James Bible, The
Gail Riplinger • AV Publications
179 pages • Available from CSE $8.25

New Age Bible Version
Gail Riplinger • AV Publications
699 pages • Available from CSE $9.50

Prophet, The
Chick Publications
32 pages • Available from CSE $2.00

Remarkable Record of Job, The
Henry Morris • Master Books
146 pages • Available from CSE $8.50

Remarkable Wisdom of Solomon, The
Henry Morris • Master Books
236 pages • Available from CSE $11.50

Who is This Allah?
G. J. O. Moshay • The Berean Call
182 pages • Available from CSE $7.50

Cancer

Arjona, David
Health Genesis
1111 Kane Concourse, Suite 303
Bay Harbor, FL 33154
(888) 301-1336, (877) 342-5217 or (305) 861-0898
fax (305) 861-8962
www.healthgenesis.com
Health related products.

Cancer Control Society
Loraine Rosenthal • 2043 North Berendo Street
Los Angeles, CA 90027 • (323) 663-7801
Also has information on multiple sclerosis.

Hallelujah Acres
P.O. Box 2388 • 900 South Post Road
Shelby, NC 28151
(704) 481-1700 / fax (704) 481-0345
www.yourlifesource.com • Health Information

International Credible Medicine Association
P.O. Box 610767 • Dallas/Fort Worth, TX 75261
(817) 481-9772 • Information on H_2O_2 Oxidative Therapy, using hydrogen peroxide to aid healing. No information given over phone; must write for information.

Power of Healing, The Power of God, The
Sardi, Bill • 475 West Allen, #117
San Dimas, CA 91773 • (909) 861-3454
www.askbillsardi.com • Information on health-related problems • 208 pages
Available from CSE $19.50

Tyler, Dr. Larry
207 West 2nd Street • Washington, MO 63090
(314) 239-2323 • Information on health problems

Vaccinations: Deception & Tragedy
Michael Dye • Hallelujah Acres Publishing
120 pages • Available from CSE $8.50

World Without Cancer
American Media • G. Edward Griffin
P.O. Box 4646 • West Lake Village, CA 91359
(800)595-6596 • Excellent book, explaining how cancer works and the politics in America that has kept natural cures from reaching the people.
368 pages • Available from CSE $17.50

Cave Men, So-Called

After the Flood
Bill Cooper • New Wine Press
256 pages • Available from CSE $12.50

Bone Peddlers, The
William R. Fix • Macmillan Pub. House
866 Third Avenue • New York, New York 10022
Excellent, documents the fact that evolutionists have no evidence for evolution. Although Mr Fix does not come all the way to the creationists' viewpoint, this 320-page book supplies ammunition for anyone wanting to refute the theory of evolution.

Bones of Contention
Marvin L. Lubenow • Best exposé of the so-called "cave men" in print today is given in this creationist assessment of human fossils. High school/adult level. 295 pages • Available from CSE $13.00

Buried Alive
Jack Cuozzo • Master Books Inc.
PO Box 727 • Green Forest, AR 72638
www.masterbooks.net • Available from CSE for $13.00

Discovery of Genesis, The
C. H. Kang and E. R. Nelson
139 pages • Available from CSE $9.50

Hidden History of the Human Race, The
Michael A. Cremo and Richard L. Thompson
Govardham Hill Publishing
P.O. Box 1920 • Alachua, FL 32615
Great book exposing cave men by (of all people)
two followers of eastern religions • 344 pages

Noah to Abram: the Turbulent Years
Erich A. von Fange
371 pages • Available from CSE $17.50

Puzzle of Ancient Man, The
Donald E. Chittick • Creation Compass
P.O. Box 993 • Newberg, OR 97132
Evidence from past cultures indicating man was
very advanced from the creation. (170 pages)
Available from CSE $10.00

Texas Tracks and Artifacts
R. Helfinstine, J. Roth
109 pages • Available from CSE $9.50

Creation Information

Alpha Omega Institute
PO Box 4343 • Grand Junction, CO 81502
(970) 523-9943 • www.discovercreation.org

American Portrait Films
PO Box 809 • Brunswick, OH 44212
(330) 220-6693 • fax (330) 220-6253
www.amport.com

Ammunition
Norm Sharbaugh • Norm Sharbaugh Ministries
PO Box 215 • Brownsburg, IN 46112
(317) 852-0877 • Covers best general arguments for
evolution, and how to refute them. Includes
interesting facts and artifacts from various fields of
science to debunk evolution.

Answers Book, The
Dr. Samuel C. Gipp • DayStar Publishing
164 pages • Available from CSE $6.50

Answers Book, The
Ken Ham, Andrew Snelling, Carl Wieland
Master Books • PO Box 726
Green Forest, AR 72638 • (800)999-3777
www.masterbooks.net•www.answersingenesis.org

Astronomy and the Bible
Donald DeYoung • ICR
176 pages • Available from CSE $9.50

Biblical Creationism
Henry M. Morris • Baker Books
PO Box 6287 • Grand Rapids, MI 49516

What each book of the Bible teaches about Creation
and the Flood. 276 pages. • www.icr.org

Bible: Key to Understanding the Early Earth, The
Southwest Radio Church
PO Box 100 • Bethany, OK 73008
(800) 652-1144 or (403) 787-2589
Great collection of evidence that the earth is not
"millions of years old." • www.swrc.com

Biblical Basis for Modern Science, The
Henry M. Morris • 10946 Woodside Avenue North
Santee, CA 92071 • (619) 448-0900 • www.icr.org
As in all of his books, Dr. Morris does a splendid job
of clearly showing science supports the Bible rather
than evolution.

Big God vs. Big Science
Bill Sardi • Here & Now Books
108 pages • Available from CSE $7.00

Bone of Contention
Sylvia Baker • Answers in Genesis
PO Box 6302 • Acacia Ridge D.C., Qld 4110
Australia • A great, must-read, short book with
loads of useful information about the creation-
evolution subject • 35 pages
Available from CSE $3.50

Book of Jasher, The
Artisan Publishers • 254 pages
Available from CSE $9.75

Claws, Jaws and Dinosaurs
Williams Gibbons and Dr. Kent Hovind
At last a cryptozoology book for young readers
from a creation perspective! Gibbons has been to
the Congo three times as well as many other
expeditions gathering evidence of the few small
dinosaurs that are still alive today. Ages seven and
up will enjoy this book. 72 pages.
Available from CSE $5.00

Comfort, Ray
Living Waters • PO Box 1172
Bellflower, CA 90706 • www.raycomfort.com
Great helps for evangelism

Creation and Time
Mark Van Bebber & Paul S. Taylor
2628 West Birchwood Circle • Mesa, AZ 85202
(800) 332-2261 • 120 pages
A great book exposing the false teaching of Hugh
Ross. •Available from CSE $6.50

Creation Student Workbook
(Homeschooler's Curriculum Notebook)
Charles Lynn, M.Ed • 58 pages
Available from CSE $8.50

Creation Scientists Answer Their Critics
10946 Woodside Avenue North
Santee, CA 92071 • (619) 448-0900
www.icr.org • 451 pages
Available from CSE $15.50

Creation's Tiny Mystery
Robert V. Gentry • A technical book about radio-polonium halos, the little marvels in granite rocks that prove the world was created instantly as the Bible says (earth never was a hot, molten mass as currently taught in secular schools). Upper high-school students and adults will gain valuable insights from this amazing work. • 363 pages
www.halos.com • Available from CSE $13.50

Darwin's Black Box
Michael J Behe • Simon & Schuster
307 pages • available from CSE $12.50

Darwin on Trial
Phillip E. Johnson • InterVarsity Press
PO Box 1400 • Downer's Grove, IL 60515
Law professor at University of California, Berkley, does a great job showing evolution is not logical.
Www.gospelcom.net/ivpress

Darwin's Enigma
Luther Sunderland • Master Books
92 pages • Available from CSE $10.50

Defeating Darwinism
Phillip Johnson • InterVarsity Press
131 pages • Available from CSE $10.50

Defender's Bible
Notes by Dr. Henry Morris • World Publishing, Inc.
(Over 6400 explanatory footnotes)
Available from CSE $30.00/$45.00

Did Adam Have a Bellybutton?
Ken Ham • Master Books
192 pages • Available from CSE $10.50

Dinosaurs by Design
Duane T. Gish, Ph.D. • Learn everything that you have ever wanted to know about dinosaurs. Where they lived, how the fossils were formed, and whether there are some still alive today.
88 pages/hardback • Available from CSE $15.50

Discovery of Genesis, The
C. H. Kang, Ethel R. Nelson • Concordia Pub. House
3558 South Jefferson Ave • St. Louis, MO 63118
Shows the connection between the Chinese language characters and the original creation. Every Chinese person needs to read this book.
135 pages • Available from CSE $9.50

Doubts About Creation? Not After This
Brian Young
191 pages • Available from CSE $9.50

Evolution: A Theory in Crisis
Michael Denton • Adler & Adler Publishers
Highly recommended. Author is not a creationist, but destroys evolution scientifically.

Evolution: Fact, Fraud, or Faith?
Don Boys, Ph.D • Freedom Publications
352 pages • Available from CSE $14.00

Fossil, Facts, and Fantasies
Joe Taylor • Mt Blanco Museum
80 pages • Available from CSE $19.50

Gap Theory, The
K. Hovind, S. Lawwell • CSE
20 pages • Available from CSE $2.00

Genesis Flood, The
J. Whitcomb, H. Morris • ICR
518 pages • Available from CSE $14.50

Genesis Solution, The
Ken Ham, Paul Taylor
Films for Christ Association
2628-A W. Birchwood Cir. • Mesa, Arizona 85202
Highly recommend, easy to read and understand for junior high age and up. • www.icr.org

God Doesn't Believe in Atheists
Ray Comfort • Living Waters
191 pages • Available from CSE $7.50

How to Make an Atheist Backslide
Ray Comfort • Bridge-Logos Publisher
219 pages • Available from CSE $5.00

Icons of Evolution
Jonathan Wells • Regnery Publishing, Inc
338 pages • Available from CSE $23.95

In the Beginning
Walt Brown • Center for Scientific Creation
5612 North 20th Place • Phoenix, AZ 85016
A thoroughly documented book about creation, the flood of Noah, and the hydroplate theory of mountain formation and continental drift.
Available from CSE $23.50

In Six Days
John Ashton • Master Books
384 pages • Available from CSE $13.50

In the Minds of Men
Ian Taylor
Well-referenced and documented, one of the best books I have ever read on the controversy of creation-evolution; any serious student of this subject needs to read it (high school/adult level).
498 pages • Available from CSE $22.50

Language of the King James, The
Gail Riplinger • A.V. Publications
179 pages • Available from CSE $8.25

Long War Against God, The
Henry M. Morris • Creation Truth Publications
P.O. Box 1435 • Noble, Oklahoma 73068
www.icr.org
One of the best books I've ever read! No other book puts things in perspective or explains how new age, pantheism, eastern religions, and evolution all tie in together quite like this one.
344 pages • Available from CSE $13.00

Men of Science—Men of God
Henry M. Morris • Master Books
P.O. Box 727• Green Forest, AR 72638
(800)999-3777)
Brief biographical sketches of some of the great men of science and how their belief in God and creation motivated their research. Junior high and up will love this book.

Origin of the Species Revisited, Vol. 1 and 2
Wendel R. Byrd • Regency (Thomas Nelson)
Nashville, Tennessee
Probably the most thorough book on this subject, 500-plus pages in each. Brilliantly argued evidence (before the Supreme Court) that the evolution theory has no scientific evidence to support it.

Panorama of Creation
Carl, E. Baugh, Ph.D.
An explanation of how the earth was different before the flood.
98 pages • Available from CSE $8.50

Reason in the Balance
Phillip E. Johnson • InterVarsity Press
P.O. Box 1400 • Downers Grove, IL 60515
The case against naturalism in science, law, and education. Excellent book.
245 pages • Available from CSE $13.50

Refuting Evolution
Jonathan Sarfati • Master Books
143 pages • Available from CSE $8.50

Revised and Expanded Answers
K. Ham, J. Srfati, C. Wieland • Master Books
274 pages • Available from CSE $11.50

Revised Quote Book, The
Institute for Creation Research • P.O. Box 2667
El Cajon, California 92021 • (619) 448-0900
Quotes by famous evolutionists admitting they have no evidence for their theory.
Available from CSE $3.50

Ride to Glory
Warren Johns • General Title Company
414 pages • Available from CSE $28.50

Science According to Moses
Dr. G. Thomas Sharp
Creation Truth Publications
P.O. Box 1435 • Noble, Oklahoma 73068
(405) 872-9856
About $15; 351 pages.

Scientific Analysis of Genesis, A
Edward F. Blick • Hearthstone Pub., Ltd.
Division of Southwest Radio Church of the Air
P.O. Box 815 • Oklahoma City, OK 73101
An engineer examines the book of Genesis.

Science and the Bible Volumes 1 and 2
Donald B. DeYoung • Baker Books
Thirty scientific demonstrations illustrating Scriptural truths. 110 pages. CSE $17.00

Scientific Creationism
Henry M. Morris• Creation-Life Publishers
P.O. Box 15666 • San Diego, CA 92115
Great overall view on the subject, has chapters on each of the main topics in the creation-evolution debate, highly recommended.
Available from CSE $9.50

Scopes II—The Great Debate
Bill Keith • Huntington House, Inc.
1200 North Market Street • Suite G
Shreveport, LA 71107
By Louisiana state senator, Bill Keith (wrote the law to require creation to be taught if evolution is taught in public schools). Covers legal battle raging over what to teach in public schools, 193 pages.

Seven Men Who Ruled the World from the Grave
Dave Breese • Moody Press
False philosophies that have affected people's thinking around the world.
235 pages • Available from CSE $11.75

Texas Tracks and Artifacts
Robert F. Helfinstine, Jerry D. Roth
1136 Fifth Avenue South • Anoka, MN 55303
(612) 421-8964
Most current book on both human and dinosaur tracks found together in Glen Rose, Texas.
109 pages • Available from CSE $9.50

That Their Words May Be Used Against Them
Henry M. Morris • Institute for Creation Research
P.O. Box 2667 • El Cajon, CA 92021
A giant book of thousands of quotes by evolutionists and famous scientists testifying that the evolution theory has no real scientific evidence to back it up. The CD-ROM that comes with the book makes it a breeze to research by topic or author. I use this book every week in research on the creation/evolution subject.
479 pages • Available from CSE $19.50

Tornado in a Junkyard
James Perloff • Refuge Books
321 pages • Available from CSE $15.00

Train Up a Child, To
Michael & Debi Pearl
Michael & Debi Pearl (published by)
109 pages • Available from CSE $4.75

Unformed and Unfilled
Weston W. Fields • Burgener Enterprises
P.O. Box 1160 • Collinsville, Illinois 62234
A critique of the Gap Theory, Day age theory and
Progressive creation.
245 pages • Available from CSE 8.00

Unknown Earth: A Handbook of Geological Enigmas
William R. Corliss • The Sourcebook Project
P.O. Box 107 • Glen Arm, Maryland 21057
(410) 668-6047 • www.science-frontiers.com
All his books are great sources of information to
show that the current theory of evolution does not
withstand close scrutiny.

Unlocking the Mysteries of Creation
Dennis Peterson • Christian Equippers, Int.
P.O. Box 16100 • South Lake Tahoe, CA 95706
(916) 542-1509 • www.equipper.com
Highly recommended. Excellent, lots of great-for-
children visuals, explains in simple language the
fallacies of evolution. Much helpful information for
those interested in the study of evolutionary theory.
237 pages • Available from CSE $24.50

World's Most Famous Court Trial
Rhea County Historical Society • Bryan College
Dayton, Tennessee 37321 • (423) 775-2041
Fascinating reading (339 pages) The actual recorded
transcript of the 1925 Scopes Monkey Trial,
showing the step-by-step trial progress. (Very
different from the movie currently making the
circuit, Inherit the Wind. If this movie is to be
shown in your public school, I strongly recommend
you protest it on the grounds that it is nothing like
the original transcript. Many changes have been
made to make creationists and Christians look
dumb.) Contact Bryan College for more information
about the trial and a good reenactment of it.

World That Perished, The
John C. Whitcomb • Baker Book House
Grand Rapids, Mich. 49506
Shows evidence for a world-wide Flood, 144 pages.

Young Earth, The
John Morris • Master Books
208 pages • Available from CSE $14.50

Young World After All, It's a
Paul D. Ackerman • Baker Book House
Grand Rapids, MI 49506
A great collection of scientific proofs that the earth
is not millions of years old.

Dinosaurs, Living Today
† includes eyewitness accounts
‡ author indicates belief in evolution

Alien Animals †‡
Janet and Colin Bord • Stackpole Books
Cameron & Kelker Streets • P.O. Box 1831
Harrisburg, PA 17105 • 215 pages

Bigfoot and Nessie: Two Mysterious Monsters †‡
Angelo Resciniti and Duane Damon
School Book Fairs, Inc. • 5093 Westerville Road
Columbus, Ohio 43229

Cadborosaurus
Dr. Paul H. LeBlond and Dr. Edward Blusfield
Horsdal & Schubart Publishers Ltd.
Victoria,B.C. Canada
134 pages • Available from CSE $9.50

Canada's Monsters
Betty Sanders Garner • Potlatch Publications
95 pages • Available from CSE $9.75

Claws, Jaws, and Dinosaurs
William Gibbons and Kent Hovind
c/o 29 Cummings Road • Pensacola, Florida [32503]
At last a cryptozoology book for young readers from
a creationist perspective! Gibbons has been to the
Congo three times as well as many other expeditions
gathering evidence of the few small dinosaurs that
are still alive. Ages eight and up will love this book.
72 pages • Available from CSE $5.00

Curious Encounters †‡
Loren Coleman • Faber and Faber, Inc.
50 Cross Street • Winchester, MA 01890

Dinosaur
Carl E. Baugh, Ph.D.
Creation Evidence Museum
P.O. Box 309 • Glen Rose, Texas 76043
(254) 897-3200 • www.creationevidence.org
Great book about the research being done in Glen
Rose, Texas, where both dinosaur and human
footprints have been found together.

Encyclopedia of Monsters, The ‡
Daniel Cohen • Dorset Press, New York
Excellent Research (as in his other books) well
worth investigating by any cryptozoologist on
subjects such as Loch Ness Monster (though a bit of
fringe approach and definite belief in evolution).
287 pages.

Enigma of Loch Ness, The
Henry H. Bauer • University of Illinois Press
243 pages.

Fossil Facts & Fantasies
Taylor, Joe
124 West Main • Crosbyton, TX 79322
(806) 675-7777 • www.mtblanco.com
Creation Museum and information on fossils.
80 pages • Available at CSE $19.50

Great Dinosaur Mystery and the Bible, The
Paul Taylor
Child's-level book about men and dinosaurs living
together, has the color picture of the plesiosaur
caught by the Japanese fishing boat in 1977.
61 pages • Available from CSE $13.95

Greatest Monsters in the World †‡
Daniel Cohen • Dodd, Mead, and Company

In Search of Lake Monsters †‡
Peter Costello • Garnstone Press Limited
59 Brompton Road • London, England SW3 IDS

In Search of Ogopogo
Arlene Gaal • Hancock House
208 pages • Available from CSE $14.50

Living Dinosaur?, A †‡
Dr. Roy P. Mackal • E. J. Brill, Leiden, Holland
Great example of the research going on in the
Congo Swamp where 25-35 foot apatosaurs still
live. Dr. Roy Mackal, University of Chicago.
340 pages • Available from CSE $29.50

Loch Ness Monster †‡
Tim Dinsdale • Routledge and Kegal Paul
9 Park Street • Boston, MA 01208

Monster Hunt
Tim Dinsdale • Acropolis Books Ltd.
Washington, DC 20009

Monster at Loch Ness †‡
Sally Berke • Raintree Publishers Limited
205 West Highland Avenue
Milwaukee, Wisconsin 53203

Monster of Loch Ness †‡
James Cornell • Scholastic Book Services
50 West 44 Street • New York, New York 10036

Monster! Monster! †‡
Betty Sanders Garner • Hancock House
19313 Zero Avenue, Surrey, BC. V4P 1M7
(604)538-1114
As the search for unknown creatures continues, this
book gives the complete story of "monsters"
(possibly living dinosaurs) that many believe live in
North America.
190 pages • Available from CSE $12.00

Mysterious America †‡
Loren Coleman • Faber and Faber, Inc.
50 Cross Street • Winchester, MA 01890

Mysterious Creatures †‡
Time-Life Books • 1450 East Parham Road
Richmond, Virginia 23280
(800)621-7026

Mysterious Sea Monsters of California's Central Coast
Randall A. Reinstedt • Ghost Town Publications
P.O. Drawer 5998 • Carmel, CA 93291
This updated version is the most complete collection of local sea monster stories ever assembled,
including many incidents related personally to the
author by the fishermen who experienced them.
(71 pages) • Available from CSE $6.50

Mysterious World
Arthur C. Clarke • Video Series • (800) 538-5856
13 tapes for about $170
This great video series has most of the known
pictures, movies, and interviews about Loch Ness
Monster, etc.

Sea Monsters †‡
William Knowlton
Alfred A. Knopf, Inc. New York, New York

On the Track of Unknown Animals †‡
Bernard Heuvelmans • The Sourcebook Project
P.O. Box 107 • Glen Arm, Maryland 21057•
A giant book of hundreds of stories about Cryptids.

Sea Serpents, Sailors, and Skeptics †‡
Graham J. McEwan • Routledge & Kegan Paul
9 Park Street • Boston, Mass. 02108

Shipwrecks and Sea Monsters of California's Central Coast
Randall A. Reinstedt • Ghost Town Publications
P.O. Drawer 5998 • Carmel, CA 93921
Documented stories of over forty shipwrecks and
the remarkable tales of strange beasts that inhabit
the submarine canyon outside Monterrey Bay. This
book contains the best known photos of the forty
foot sea serpent that washed up on a California
beach in 1925. 168 pages.
Available from CSE $9.00

Unexplained!
Jerome Clark • Visible Ink Press
835 Penobscot Bldg. • Detroit, Michigan 48226
A catalog of 347 strange sightings and puzzling
physical phenomena.
443 pages • Available from CSE $8.50

Mark of the Beast

The MARK of the New World Order
Terry L. Cook • Second Coming Ministries
61535 S. Highway 97 • Unit 9, Suite 288
Bend, Oregon 97702
Reveals the hidden agenda of those who are pushing loss of privacy and biochip technology. 385 pages.

Martin, Dean
(850) 455-5011 • martindl@freent.com
Speaks on and demonstrates embeddable microchip technology.

Trumpet Ministries
www.trumpetmin.org • sho-phar@trumpetmn.org
He helped invent the implant chip.

New Age Movement

Ancient Empires of the New Age
Paul DeParrie and Mary Pride
Fascinating, covers some of the history of the New Age Movement and shows a little bit about what is happening today to bring us back to the Satanic New World Order, 201 pages.

Citizen's Rule Book
Paper-House Publications
62 pages • Available from CSE $1.00

En Route to Global Occupation
Gary H. Kah • Huntington House Publishers
P.O. Box 53788 • Lafayette, Louisiana 70505
One of the best books on the New Age movement, exposing what is happening today as we race toward the one-world order of which Satan will be the head, 213 pages.

Foundations of Liberty
Texe Marrs • Living Truth Ministries
1708 Patterson Road • Austin, Texas 78733
(800) 234-9673 • www.texemarrs.com
$20+$3.50 P&H.

Fourth Reich of the Rich
Des Griffin • Emissary Publications
316 pages • Available from CSE $11.00

Hushmoney
Peter Kershaw • Heal Our Land Ministries
208 E. College Steet, Suite 262 • Branson, MO 65616
(417) 337-7533 (Voice Mail) • www.hushmoney.org
A must-read for pastors and ministry leaders. Exposes the hidden dangers of 501 (c) (3) Incorporation. 46 pages • Available at CSE $5.00

In Caesar's Grip
Peter Kershaw • Heal Our Land Ministries
141 pages • Available from CSE $15.00

In the Minds of Men
Ian T. Taylor • TFE Publishing
498 pages • Available from CSE $25.00

Now is the Dawning of the New World Order
Dennis Lawrence Cuddy, Ph.D.
Hearthstone Pub., Ltd. • P.O. Box 815
Oklahoma City, OK 73101
Good, fast-paced, filled with information on the New Age Movement. With 415 pages, it will answer all the questions you have and even raise a few more.

New Age Bible Versions
Riplinger, Gail • A. V. Publications
PO Box 280 • Ararat, VA 24053
(540) 251-1734 / fax (540) 251-1734
www.jesusislord.com/riplinge.htm
Information on Bible versions
699 pages •Available from CSE $9.50

New Age Movement Seminar
Gary Frye, Evangelist • 809 Oriole Lane
Concord, NC 28025 • (704) 782-5273
Personal friend of mine, very knowledgeable about the New Age Movement, travels to churches and speaks on this topic (much as I do on Creation). Your church would greatly profit from his seminar.

On the Horns of the Beast
Bill Still • Reinhardt & Still Pub.
4250 Cedar Creek Grade
Winchester, Virginia 22602
The history of the Federal Reserve and the disappearance of America's gold reserves. 312 pages.

7 Men Who Rule the World from the Grave
Dave Breese • Moody Press
235 pages •Available from CSE $11.75

Shadows of Power, The
James Perloff • Western Islands Publishers
264 pages • Available from CSE $10.50

Noah's Ark

Discovered: Noah's Ark
Ron Wyatt
www.wyattmuseum.com
World Bible Society • Nashville, TN 37203
I have met with Ron and seen much of the evidence he presents.

Noah's Ark Pitched and Parked
Nathan M. Meyer
Nathan Meyer Bible Prophecy Association
190 Loveman Avenue
Worthington, Ohio 43085

Public Schools and Evolution

Are You Being Brainwashed?
Dr. Kent Hovind • Creation Science Evangelism
36 pages • Available from CSE $2.00

Elizabeth Ridenour
National council on bible curriculum in Public Schools
PO Box 9743 • Greensboro, NC 27429
(336) 272-3799 • www.bibleinschools.org

Of Pandas and People
Davis & Kenyon • Haughton Publishing
Company
170 pages • Available from CSE $17.50

Students Legal Rights on a Public School Campus
J. W. Brinkley • Roever Communications
P.O. Box 136130 • Fort Worth, Texas 76136
(817) 238-2005
Explains what rights religious students have in public schools.
119 pages • Available from CSE $9.50

Teaching Creation Science in Public Schools
Duane T. Gish • Institute for Creation Research
P.O. Box 2667 • El Cajon, California 92021
Every public school teacher needs this book.
70 pages • Available from CSE $4.75

Textbooks on Trial
James C. Hefley • Victor Books • P.O. Box 1825
Wheaton, Illinois 60187
Highly recommended, covers the battle going on in public school textbooks today (193 pages).

What Are They Teaching Our Children?
Mel and Norma Gabler
Educational Research Analysts • P.O. Box 7518
Longview, Texas 75607 • (903) 753-5993
Fax (903) 753-7788
Great book to show the humanist influence in today's textbooks.
192 pages • Available from CSE $4.00

Your Rights in the Public Schools
John C. Whitehead • The Rutherford Institute
P.O. Box 7482 • Charlottesville, VA 22906
(800) 441-3473
Must-read booklet (26 pages) dealing with the students' and parents' legal rights in the public school system.
35 pages • Available from CSE 3.00

The Rights of Religious Persons in Public Education
John W. Whitehead • Crossway Books
Good News Publishers • Wheaton, IL 60187

Pyramid

Great Pyramid—Prophecy in Stone
Noah W. Hutchings • Hearthstone Pub., Ltd.
Oklahoma City, Oklahoma
171 pages.

New Light on the Great Pyramid
N. W. Hutchings • Hearthstone Publishing
Southwest Radio Church • P.O. Box 1144
Oklahoma City, OK 73101 • (405) 789-1222

Related Topics

America—To Pray? or not to Pray?
David Barton • WallBuilder Press
P.O. Box 397 • Aledo, Texas 76008
(817) 441-6044
The effects on America from removal of prayer in the public schools. 163 pages

Education and the Founding Fathers
David Barton • Wallbuilders
P.O. Box 397 • Aledo, Texas 76008
(817)441-6044
Video

Faith and Freedom
Mathew Staver • Liberty Counsel
561 pages • Available from CSE $15.00

"Federal" Reserve Conspiracy & Rockefeller, The
Emmanuel M. Josephson • Chedney Press
230 E. 61 Street • New York, New York 10021
374 pages

Hitler's Cross
Erwin W. Lutzer • Moody Press
Chicago, Illinois 60610
216 pages

Jonah and Micah
J. Vernon McGee • Through the Bible Books
Box 7100 • Pasadena, California 91109
Consider this book for documented information of eyewitness accounts (pages 40-41) of people, dogs, or animals being swallowed by a whale (regarding the validity of Jonah's story).

Truth about Rockefeller, The
Mrs. Theo Meves • 18310 Benington Drive
Brothfield, Wisc. 53045
Excellent book about the Rockefeller dynasty's link to the New World Order. 277 pages

Understanding the Times
David A. Noebel • Harvest House Publishers
Eugene, Oregon 97402
891 pages.

Stars, Gospel in the

Heavens Declare, The
William D. Banks • Impact Christian Books
www.impactchristianbooks.com

Hieroglyphics of the Heavens, The
Carr-Harris, Bertha • Armac Press, 1933
Toronto, CANADA

Many Infallible Proofs
Henry M. Morris • Creation-Life Publishers
www.masterbooks.net

Real Meaning of the Zodiac, The
D. James Kennedy, Ph.D • Coral Ridge Ministries
5555 North Federal Hwy
Fort Lauderdale, FL 33302

Witness of the Stars
E. W. Bullinger • Kregal 1893, 1967
Grand Rapids, Michigan
www.philogos.org

UFOs

Alien Encounters
Chuck Missler • Mark Eastman • Koinonia House
P.O. Box D • Coeur d'Alene, ID 83816-0347
"This book may be one of the most disturbing books
you'll read in a long while, but it may also be one of
the most critical." –from the title page.

The Cosmic Conspiracy
Stan Deyo
Barnes & Noble ISBN# 0908477-04-4
Fascinating book about electro-gravitic propulsion,
contending that there are two types of UFOs. One
would be top-secret craft owned and operated by the
U. S. Government using a different means of propulsion called electro-gravitics. The second type of UFO he
claims are Satanically owned and operated. (For more
on this see my Creation Seminar Videotape 7)

UFO: End-Time Delusion
David Allen Lewis & Robert Shreckhise
New Leaf Press • P.O. Box 726
Green Forest, Arkansas 72638
David Lewis presents the results of 39 years of research
on UFOs.

UFO 666
David Allen Lewis & Robert Shreckhise
Menorah Press
304 East Farm Road 186 • Springfield, MO 65810
(800) 772-5687 • www.davidallenlewis.com
Cults and Contacts of the antichrist delusion.

Recommended Reading for Kids

A is for Adam
D is for Dinosaurs
Ken and Malley Ham • Master Books
An A to Z rhyme book filled with colorful
cartoon   illustrations that teach
the true history of the world.
A is for Adam is a sequel to D is for Dinosaurs.
121 pages • Available from CSE $15.50 each

Astronomy Book, The
Geology Book, The
Weather Book, The
John Morris • Master Books
This book starts with the "big picture." our
place in   space, and explains how
each of the various weather
conditions play a role in our daily lives. This book
is the   first in a series that
honors God as Creator.
80 pages • Available from CSE $15.50 each

Champions of Science
Champions of Mathematics
Champions of Invention
John Tiner • Eabon Design and Master Books
In this book, we learn that inventors like
Charles   Babbage (computers),
Michael Faraday (electric
generator), and John Gutenberg (printing press)
gave   credit for their achieve-
ments to God.
72 pages • Available from CSE $5.50 each

Claws, Jaws, & Dinosaurs
by William Gibbons and Dr. Kent Hovind
At last a cryptozoology book for young
readers from a creation perspective! Gibbons
has been to the Congo three times as well as
many other expeditions gathering evidence of
the few small dinosaurs that are still alive
today. Ages seven and up will enjoy this
book. 72 pages
Available from CSE $5.00

Dinosaurs by Design
by Duane T. Gish, Ph.D.
Learn everything that you have ever wanted
to know about dinosaurs. Where they lived,
how the fossils were formed, and whether
there are some still alive today.
88 pages/hardback
Available from CSE $13.50

Daddy, Is There Really a God?
J. Morris, K. Ham
31 pages • Available from CSE $11.50

Dinosaurs of Eden
Ken Ham
64 pages • Available from CSE $13.50

Dry Bones and Other Fossils
Gary and Mary Parker
80 pages • Available from CSE $12.50

God Created the Dinosaurs of the World
God Created the World and the Universe
Paul Taylor • Master Books
High-quality dinosaur stickers make these special coloring books particularly engaging for small children. Full of creation and dinosaur facts, these books will keep children busy for hours.
Pages • Available from CSE $4.50

God's Dinosaur 1-2-3 Book
God's Dinosaur Fun Book
God's Dinosaur A-B-C Book
God's Dinosaur Color Book
These unique books are terrific tools for helping to teach young children about shapes, colors, letters, and dinosaurs.
171 pages • Available from CSE $2.75 each

Great Dinosaur Mystery, The
by Paul S. Taylor
This unusual book presents dinosaurs as part of God's wonderful creation and uses them to introduce important Biblical concepts. 63 pages/hardback
Available from CSE $13.50

Special Wonders of Our Sea World
Special Wonders of Our Wild Kingdom
Special Wonders of Our Feathered Friend
Buddy and Kay Davis • Master Books
80 pages • Available from CSE $12.50 each

Science and the Bible
by Donald B. DeYoung
A total of sixty (thirty per volume) scientific demonstrations that illustrate Scriptural truths. These demonstrations are easy to do and use ordinary household items.
Available from CSE $13.50

Patch the Pirate: The Evolution Revolution - Audiotape
Ron Hamilton •
Patch the Pirate visits the university, where a meeting of Apeman International is being held. A suspected kidnapping sends Patch and his crew propelling back to the beginning of time. A great musical adventure on audiocassette for children ages six and up.
76 minutes • Available from CSE $9.95

Timothy Whale's Rainbow
Darrell Wiskur • Master Books
A simple, rhyming children's book that explains the flood of Noah to young children in a format that is comparable in quality to top commercial or secular projects, both in artwork, and writing.
Available from CSE $11.50

Voyage to the Planets
R. Bliss and D. DeYoung • ICR
111 pages • Available from CSE $11.50

Voyage to the Stars
R. Bliss
This book beautifully illustrates astronomy for junior-high-age students, written in th eform of an adventurous trip into space on a space shuttle. The creative disign and power of God are made evident throughout.
111 pages • Available from CSE $9.50

What Really Happened to the Dinosaurs?
by John Morris and Ken Ham
Join Tracker John and DJ as they explore the world before Noah's Flood. Kids will love the fun-filled adventure and parents will appreciate the Biblical scientific teaching.
32 pages • Available from CSE $11.00

Creation Notes:

1. Rings of Saturn:

Saturn's entire ring structure is very complex and difficult to explain via evolution. One of the rings, the "F" ring (see picture) has an intricate, unstable "braiding" feature that leaves evolutionists at a loss when trying to describe how this could have persisted for more than a few thousand years.

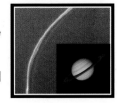

For more information about the young age of the earth and solar system, see *In The Beginning* and Creation Seminar Part One.

2. Radio-Polonium Halos:

Perfectly concentric halos that formed around radioactive elements in igneous rock (granite and other) prove that the Earth was never a hot, molten mass as evolutionists claim.

For more information read *Creation's Tiny Mystery*.

3. Symbioses:

Around the world, we find countless sets of creatures and plants that cannot exist and/or reproduce without the other, thus invalidating the theory that these organisms developed separately over millions of years.

Examples: Clown fish and sea anemones,
Yucca plants and yucca moths,
Termites and their parasites.

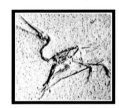

For more information, see *In the Beginning*.

4. Massive Fossil Graveyards:

There are many facts that point to rapid, catastrophic conditions which killed without warning.
• Large groups of iguanodons killed simultaneously.
• Fossilized creatures found eating each other.
• Marine mammals, including whales, found in huge deposits of dead diatoms.

For more information see Creation Seminar Part Six.

5. Global Catastrophe:

Around the world, we find enormous sedimentary rock (rock that is formed in proving that at one time the earth was water. Signs of massive runoff, such as Canyon, show that it happened quickly.

For more information see Creation Seminar Part

6. Unusual Rock Layers:

Polystrate fossils, transposed rock lay to the geologic column), and millions of petrified clams—none of these are expl evolution.

For more information see Creation Seminar Part

7. Coal Beds:

Human objects, such as the bell pict found inside coal beds prove that huma before the formation of coal.

For more details and other objects found inside Creation Seminar Part Two.

8. Oil Deposits:

Oil is frequently found at extremely It is not possible for the rock to have co pressure for millions of years; therefore formed recently and under great pressu the deposits indicates that they must ha produced in a recent catastrophe like N

For more information see Creation Seminar Part

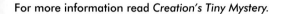

Evolution Notes:

1. Big Bang:

Scientists have tried to recreate the events of the big bang via computer simulations, but have not been able to without disregarding basic natural laws. Some try to point out select natural phenomena and claim "proof" of the big bang, but fail to realize how little science their theories actually employ.

For more information about the Big Bang, see Creation Seminar Part One.

2. Formation of the Earth:

The Second Law of Thermodynamics everything tends toward disorder. Every theory that describes this event violates Merely adding energy does not negate

For more information, see Creation Seminar Par

3. Formation of Life:

If a car can't form by chance, how co cell spontaneously form when each cell, more complex than the Space Shuttle?

For more information, see *Darwin's Black Box* an Seminar Part Four.

Most of the books and videotapes referenced on this chart are available from Creation Science Evangelism • 29 Cummings Road

layers of
water),
overed in
e Grand

Six.

ers (according
closed,
inable by

Four.

red here,
s existed

al beds, see

high pressures.
tained this
the oil was
e. The size of
ve been
ah's Flood.

One.

9. Red Sea Crossing:

Some claim that naturally occurring wind caused the water to became shallow enough for the Israelites to walk across. However, The Bible is very specific, saying that they crossed on **dry** ground while a pillar of cloud prevented Pharaoh's army from attacking the Israelites.

For more information see Exodus 13-15, www.wyattmuseum.com, and Creation Seminar Part Seven.

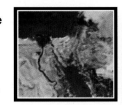

10. Jesus:

Jesus Christ is the one and only bridge between God and man. There is no other way a Holy God could save his creation from their sinful ways than by sacrificing His only begotten Son. Those who do not believe in God and repent of their sins will be judged.

The best of source of information about Jesus is the Bible.

11. Rome Falls:

The Roman Empire provided a communication and transportation system that enabled a "civilized" Europe. This culture was a sort of "collective intelligence" that was the essence of the empire, more so than the government or army. When barbarians finally destroyed Rome, there was no longer an effective way to share information. Without this collective intelligence, chaos was inevitable, and the Dark Ages resulted.

12. Gutenberg:

With the invention of the printing press, people were able to share knowledge with unprecedented ease. This rejuvenation of collective knowledge brought about a cultural revolution that catapulted Europe to be the dominating force in the world for centuries. Massive improvements in complexity and order are not possible without equally massive improvements in intelligence.

---

states that
evolutionary
this law.
his fact.

One.

uld a "simple"
by itself, is

d Creation

4. Man Appears:

Science proves that humans can only produce humans, dogs only produce dogs, and trees only produce trees. There are no missing links.

For more information see *Bones of Contention* and Creation Seminar Part Four.

5. Present:

At this point in history, information is more easily accessible than at any other time, yet many people continue to reject the truth. Unfortunately, this is reflected in all aspects of life.

For more information see Creation Seminar Part Five.

 • Pensacola, Florida [32503] • (850) 479-3466 • fax: (850) 479-8562 • web: www.drdino.com • email: dino@drdino.com